Saints Celebrated and Unsung

Saints Celebrated and Unsung

The Universal Call to Holiness

James J. Bacik

ORBIS BOOKS
Maryknoll, New York

Founded in 1970, Orbis Books endeavors to publish works that enlighten the mind, nourish the spirit, and challenge the conscience. The publishing arm of the Maryknoll Fathers and Brothers, Orbis seeks to explore the global dimensions of the Christian faith and mission, to invite dialogue with diverse cultures and religious traditions, and to serve the cause of reconciliation and peace. The books published reflect the views of their authors and do not represent the official position of the Maryknoll Society. To learn more about Orbis Books, please visit our website at www.orbisbooks.com.

Library of Congress Cataloging-in-Publication Data

Names: Bacik, James J., 1936- author.
Title: Saints celebrated and unsung : the universal call to holiness / James J. Bacik.
Description: Maryknoll, NY : Orbis Books, [2021] | Includes bibliographical references. | Summary: "Saints Celebrated and Unsung, reflects on eight general principles from Gaudete et Exultate (On the Call to Holiness in Today's World) by Pope Francis"— Provided by publisher.
Identifiers: LCCN 2020036524 (print) | LCCN 2020036525 (ebook) | ISBN 9781626984059 (trade paperback) | ISBN 9781608338696 (epub)
Subjects: LCSH: Francis, Pope, 1936- Gaudete et exsultate. | Holiness—Catholic Church. | Perfection—Religious aspects—Catholic Church. | Christian life—Catholic authors. | Catholic Church—Doctrines.
Classification: LCC BX2350.5.C383 B33 2021 (print) | LCC BX2350.5.C383 (ebook) | DDC 234/.8—dc23
LC record available at https://lccn.loc.gov/2020036524
LC ebook record available at https://lccn.loc.gov/2020036525

For Eileen H. Simon

My good friend and respected Jungian analyst;
body-energy practitioner with a remarkable healing touch;
author of the scholarly, deeply personal and culturally
significant book, Lady Underground's Gift:
Liberating the Soul within Us, *which brings to*
light the often-eclipsed feminine dimension
of the Gracious Mystery.

Contents

Foreword

For over thirty years I taught theology to undergraduate students at Boston College. My year-long course was called simply "Catholicism." One section of the course was entitled "Called to Holiness" (echoing "The Call of the Whole Church to Holiness" from *Lumen Gentium*, the Vatican II's document, Constitution on the Church). I would begin that section by inviting the students to name and explain their understanding of "holiness."

The typical response was a cascade of negative stereotypes. Their image was of "having to go to church" all the time, of saying a lot of long-winded prayers, of always being nice but boring, of pretending to be a holy Joe or Jane in front of grandparents, and generally being no fun at all. They imagined that trying to be holy would greatly cramp their present lifestyles and lose them many friends. I suspect the response of my undergrads would be fairly similar for typical adult Catholics as well—if they were being as honest!

Now, there are many reasons why holiness has had such bad press, and one of them, surely, is the kinds of saints that the church has canonized across the centuries. Things have improved a little with recent popes, but we have a long way to go to get beyond the usual pattern of requirements for sainthood, often to found a religious order or get oneself killed for the faith.

When celebrating the feast days of great saints, the old Roman Missal (used up to Vatican II) recognized them within a list of categories. Some favored designations were martyr, virgin, or virgin martyr (real achievement), and then the Missal had a catch-all category, *neither virgin nor martyr*. This was the designation for the rare canonized saints who had spouses and raised families, like Bridget of Sweden or Elizabeth of Hungary. It was as if identifying them as "married" or "parents" might detract from their witness to holiness.

The church's original instinct to raise up saints to model holiness for the rest of us was a very valid one. It is important to understand what true holiness entails for Christians and then to have models who can help us imagine our own path. Fr. Jim Bacik gives us both in spades here, describing attractively the life of Christian holiness and then raising up models of it being lived; some are from among the celebrated and others are more local to his life.

Josef Goldbrunner (1910–2003), an eminent twentieth-century theologian, wrote a short but classic book entitled *Holiness Is Wholeness*. In many ways, the title said it all. Fr. Jim Bacik echoes the same sentiment here with what deserves to become another classic. And while Jim is inspired by Pope Francis and his apostolic exhortation *Gaudete et Exultate* ("On the Call to Holiness in Today's World"), his primary model for holiness throughout is Jesus.

Turning to Jesus as our core model of holiness would seem self-evident to Christians—and is surely the right place to start. Add to this that contemporary New Testament scholarship is enabling us to recognize more reliably than ever the values and commitments of the historical Jesus. His life praxis for the reign of God must ever define the core of Christian faith and how we understand its call to holiness of life. And as the dogmas of our faith attest, this one person was both human and divine, with that carpenter from Nazareth modeling for us *the way* into holiness of life and then the Christ of faith and the paschal mystery of his death and resurrection lending us what St. Paul constantly names as "an abundance of grace" (Romans 5:17, etc.) to empower us to so live.

Jesus models for us a life of holiness that invites us to imitate his "way, truth, and life" (John 14:6). Such a life is its own reward *now*, enabling us to become the best possible people we can be, and this not just for our own sake but, as with Jesus, "for the life of the world" (John 6:51). Sociologists tell us that a primary quest of young people today is to become authentic human persons, living with personal integrity and social mutuality. There is no surer path to such holiness and wholeness than *the way* mapped and modeled by Jesus.

Jesus's *way* is best summarized in his greatest commandment—to love God by loving neighbors as ourselves, even enemies. Then throw in his parable of the Good Samaritan (Luke 10:25–37), which Aquinas described as "the Gospel in miniature," and we know that Christian holiness after *the way* of Jesus must include the works of compassion and justice. This is exactly the vision that Jim Bacik lays out in this beautiful book, crafted particularly for our time.

I promise you, *Saints Celebrated and Unsung* will lend you a fresh sense of your baptismal calling to holiness of life after *the way* of Jesus. As needed as ever, it poses models to inspire your own unique path and will prompt you to remember your own unsung saints. Fr. Jim concludes with eight wise signposts and principles to guide us along *the way*—that he has walked long and well himself.

Thinking back to those undergrads I tried to teach, this book might even make holiness attractive to such young people, appealing especially to their hearts as they long for authenticity as persons, with integrity toward themselves and mutuality with all. I've no doubt that by God's grace this book can renew all of our journeys toward holiness and wholeness of life. And as Irenaeus promised (writing circa 175), the more we come into such fullness of life, the more we give glory to God. What a gift!

Thomas Groome
Professor of Theology and Religious Education
Boston College,
author of *Faith for the Heart:*
A "Catholic" Spirituality (Paulist, 2019)

Introduction

This book is inspired by the 2018 apostolic exhortation of Pope Francis, *Gaudete et Exultate* ("On the Call to Holiness in Today's World"), which the pope intended not as a theological treatise on holiness but as a modest effort "to repropose the call to holiness in a practical way for our own time, with all its risks, challenges, and opportunities" (no. 2). The exhortation, as it will be referred to throughout, is divided into five chapters: The Call to Holiness; Subtle Enemies of Holiness; the Light of the Master; Signs of Holiness in Today's World; and Vigilance and Discernment. In this exhortation, Francis functions as a wise spiritual guide, offering acute analyses of human existence and solid practical advice for all Christians seeking to live the gospel.

In my two previous books on Pope Francis, I recognized that his role as a spiritual and pastoral guide was reinforced by his personal witness and the practical character of his teaching.[1] In this book, the pope's role as a

---

1. James Bacik, *Pope Francis and Campus Ministry* (Mahwah, NJ: Paulist Press, 2019); and *Pope Francis and His Critics* (Mahwah, NJ: Paulist Press, 2020).

spiritual director is highlighted by drawing eight general principles from his exhortation and devoting a chapter to each one. Following the conviction that personal witness makes the gospel more credible and attractive, I include two stories in each chapter, one of a celebrated saint, such as Augustine and Thérèse of Lisieux; the other of an "unsung saint," known to me personally. My presentation of these saints—both celebrated and unsung—is inspired by the theology of the German Jesuit Karl Rahner, by my almost six decades of pastoral ministry as a priest of the Diocese of Toledo, Ohio, and by my critical studies of Pope Francis.

The first chapter, which repeats the pope's insistence that we are all called to holiness, recalls the conversion of the great saint and theologian Augustine of Hippo, and is complemented by the story of Sue, who lived her faith for years as a loving wife and mother and later extended her loving care to the elderly in a nursing home. The second chapter deals with finding our unique path to holiness through the stories of the popular spiritual writer Henri Nouwen and of Bill, who totally redirected his life in his late thirties. The next chapter presents Thérèse of Lisieux and my father, George Bacik, as models of serving God through ordinary everyday activities. The fourth chapter raises up the theologian Karl Rahner, along with a parishioner, June, both of whom continued to grow in their understanding of Christ and their commitment to his teaching as they got older. The fifth chapter notes that authentic Christian spirituality must include working for justice and presents the life of Martin Luther King Jr., along with my personal priest friend Bernie Boff, who marched in Selma. The sixth chapter relates the stories of the late secretary-general of the United Nations Dag Hammarskjöld, and of Mary, both of whom met the challenges of their busy lives by maintaining a vibrant contemplative spirit. The next chapter tells the stories of two religious women, Mother Teresa and my lifelong friend Pat, a Sister of Mercy, both of whom exemplify the Lord's command to care for the needy. The final chapter considers the pope's emphasis on discernment, where we recall the conversion of the recently canonized John Henry Newman and learn of the story of a former parishioner, Charmaine, who made good decisions leading to a happy marriage. The conclusion summarizes the eight major principles for spiritual growth and offers some advice on how to implement each of them.

1

All Called to Holiness

"We are frequently tempted to think that holiness is only for those who can withdraw from ordinary affairs to spend much time in prayer. That is not the case. We are all called to be holy by living our lives with love and by bearing witness in everything we do, wherever we find ourselves" (no. 14). This is the message Pope Francis addresses to all of us in his 2018 apostolic exhortation, *Gaudete et Exultate* ("On the Call to Holiness in Today's World"). Francis insists that the Lord "wants us to be saints and not to settle for a bland and mediocre existence" (no. 1). Recognizing a potential problem, he encourages us: "Do not be afraid of holiness," because "it will take away none of your energy, vitality or joy" but will set you free from "every form of enslavement," move you to become your "deepest self" and recognize your "great dignity" (no. 32).

The pope's appeal to seek holiness and to become a saint resonates with some Christians today, especially those inclined to see saints as role models and those attuned to the church's teaching on the universal call to holiness. At the same time, there are many good Christians who generally think in more secular terms and do not respond well to the religious language of "sainthood," perhaps finding it too lofty, unrealistic, ethereal, or out of reach. We need other ways to interest those more secularized Christians in the many good ideas Pope Francis presents in his inspiring exhortation.

One possibility is to frame the pope's teaching as a path to greater personal growth, deeper self-actualization, and more generous service, notions that can be found in his exhortation. We could also borrow language from the world of athletics, where coaches and players commonly talk about improving day by day, getting steadily better and learning from defeats. This approach to spiritual growth could be applied to major life transitions; for example, a young woman could strive to achieve a healthier attitude toward sexuality as she prepares for marriage, or an older man could try to gain a deeper appreciation of leisure in preparation for retirement. We could apply it to the liturgical year: by the end of Advent, I want to be a more patient person; or when Pentecost ends the Easter season, I hope to have a more joyful sense of my faith. On a daily basis, we could include in our night prayers a brief review of any progress we made that day on our spiritual journey. Christians broadly interested in making progress in the spiritual life can join those committed to sainthood in appropriating the sage advice of Francis in his apostolic exhortation.

Fundamentally, the pope encourages all of us to determine the next step forward on the spiritual journey and to take it now. For some, that step might be obvious, as in the case of the alcoholic who needs to join AA and go to meetings regularly. For others, determining the most helpful step forward may be more difficult, requiring prayerful discernment or advice from confidant, sometimes revealing, unexpected approaches; for example, a mother struggling to be the adult in dealing with her teenage daughter may find that regular exercise, which gives her more energy, is more helpful than daily prayer. Procrastination can be a serious impediment to spiritual growth. It may help to take at least a tiny step toward a desired goal; for instance, a person who knows it would be good to say a prayer every day before going to work could start out by doing it at least a couple times a week.

A Celebrated Saint

Francis encourages us to learn from the example of the great canonized saints. On the call to holiness, Augustine of Hippo (354–430) offers helpful advice in his classic autobiography, *Confessions*, which is a popular way to encounter the man and his thought. His autobiographical style resonates with many people today, as do his vivid descriptions of common human experiences: joys and sorrows, virtues and sins, deep desires and failed dreams, spiritual delights and intense grief. Augustine started working on the *Confessions* in 397, when he was forty-three years old and at the beginning of his long tenure as bishop of Hippo, a seacoast town in Northern Africa (modern-day Algeria) with an estimated population of thirty thousand people. As a relatively new bishop of the minority Catholic community, Augustine was under attack from two sides. The majority Christian group in Hippo and large parts of North Africa, known as the Donatists, assailed him as the leader of a heretical community that had faltered under persecution in the past and was now too submissive to the Roman Empire and too lax in the practice of the faith.

A Former Manichean

Some members of the Catholic community in North Africa also distrusted Augustine because of his well-known association with the Manicheans, which started when he was in Carthage at age seventeen and lasted over a decade. The followers of Mani thought of themselves as Christians but did not accept the Old Testament, the death of Jesus on the cross, or the legitimacy of Baptism and the Eucharist. Augustine's baptism had occurred far away in Milan, Italy, and the North African Catholic community had doubts about the authenticity of his conversion. Some felt he was still a Manichean at heart.

Given this background, many scholars are convinced that Augustine wrote his *Confessions* to defend himself against these personal attacks. In recalling the story of his life up to his baptism and the death of his mother, Monica, in 388, he does play down his involvement with the

Manicheans and explicitly expresses his disappointment with their great teacher Faustus. He does not even mention the Donatists, even though in 397 much of his energy as a bishop went into defending his community against their sharp and sometimes violent attacks. Instead, he concentrates on more personal matters, such as his inner struggles against temptation.

Monica

The way Augustine weaves his mother, Monica, into his life story is intriguing and revealing. He portrays her as a prototype of the contemporary helicopter parent. Being a good Christian, she instructed her son in the ways of the faith, although she followed the customs of her community and did not have him baptized. Chafing under her domineering ways, Aurelius, as he was named, was relieved to leave home to study when he was eleven. Five years later, he was forced to return home and absorbed from his mother "enormous anxiety," which affected his relationship with women. After a brief stay, he went to Carthage, where he entered into what we might call a common-law marriage with a woman he never names, and fathered a son named Adeodatus. Contrary to common misconceptions, he was faithful to his lower-social-class wife during their fifteen years together. When Augustine returned to his hometown, Tagaste, to teach in 375, Monica would, at first, not let him into her house because he had become a

Manichean, relenting only after she had a dream indicating he would one day return to the true faith. When he decided to go to Rome to further his career as a professor of rhetoric, Monica followed him to the coast, where "she clung to me, passionately determined that I should either go back home with her or take her to Rome." To get away from her, he lied about a friend in need and during the night stole away, carrying with him severe guilt feelings.

Conversion

After a miserable year teaching in Rome, Augustine went to Milan, where the imperial court resided. Monica joined him there and forced him to dismiss his wife to open the way for a more profitable marriage that would further his career. Augustine later wrote that saying goodbye to his wife "was a blow which crushed my heart to bleeding. I loved her dearly." In Milan, Augustine underwent a conversion process, prompted by various forces: listening to the preaching of Bishop Ambrose; encountering an intellectually satisfying synthesis of Neoplatonic philosophy and Christianity; hearing the stories of dedicated ascetical monks; and especially reading a passage from Paul calling him to put aside lust and to put on Christ (Rom 13:13–14), which unleashed a flood of tearful emotion within him. This experience led to his baptism by Ambrose at the Easter Vigil in 387. Monica was thrilled; and, afterward, she and her son went to Ostia, where they enjoyed together a deep religious experience. They were looking at a garden through a window while talking of God's Wisdom and then, for one ecstatic instant, they touched "Divine Wisdom" before returning to their normal conversation. Within a few weeks, Monica was dead. Near the end of the autobiographical section of *Confessions*, Augustine recalled, "my soul was wounded, my very life torn asunder, for it had been one life—made of hers and mine together."

Confessions

The *Confessions* may be a clever defense of Augustine's orthodoxy; it is also a profound psychological analysis of the ways he resisted the divine call but then finally succumbed to God's persistence. Reflecting on his earlier conversion experience, Augustine addresses God in the tenth book of his *Confessions*: "Late have I loved you, O Beauty ever ancient and ever new: late have I loved you." He recognizes his fundamental error: "And see, you were within and I was in the external world and sought you there, and in my unlovely state I plunged into those lovely created things which you made." Along the same line: "You were with me and I was not with you." Recognizing God's persistence and power: "You called and cried out loud and shattered my deafness. You were radiant and resplendent, you put to flight my blindness." And then comes his own response: "I tasted you, and I feel but hunger and thirst for you. You touched me, and I am set on fire to attain the peace which is yours."

Application

Augustine's remarkable reflection on his conversion reminds us of Francis Thompson's *The Hound of Heaven*, where God pursues us down the "labyrinthine ways" of our minds, never tires of forgiving us, and ceaselessly seeks to touch our minds and hearts. Augustine's story invites us to look for God within, for God is closer to us than we are to ourselves. It also alerts us to ways—perhaps subtle, hard to detect, and easily rationalized—that we may be blocking the call to holiness. For example, a practicing Catholic who actively participates in the Sunday liturgy may automatically tune out any applications to social justice made in the homily. Indirectly, Augustine teaches us that it is never too late to respond to the divine call to holiness. Loving late is less than ideal, but it is better than not loving at all. We should take a step toward greater spiritual maturity now, without delay, but today's failure leaves open tomorrow's possibilities. Procrastination is dangerous to spiritual health, but it need not be fatal. A wife who realizes she has endured a psychologically abusive marriage far too long may benefit from waiting a few more weeks or months to gather herself and develop an effective strategy before confronting her husband with a demand that they see a marriage counselor together.

A Caution

We need to be cautious in reflecting on Augustine's portrayal of the inner peace he felt in his conversion experience. We cannot expect or demand such a gift as we respond to the call of holiness. It is true, however, that ordinary people who make choices in tune with God's will often do experience some sort of consolation, perhaps a quiet assurance of being on the right road or a simple conviction that no more soul searching is necessary. A man who, for a long time, anxiously rejected the impulse to reconcile with his estranged sister finally decided to call her and slept better that night. However, there are times when individuals, following a dictate of their well-formed conscience, take a proper step forward without any sense of consolation or satisfaction but with feelings of dread and foreboding. For instance, a woman did the right thing in standing up for a Muslim co-worker who was periodically subjected to Islamophobic comments, even though her good deed went unappreciated, drew the ire of one of her friends, and failed to reward her with any sense of satisfaction. Sometimes, the appropriate step forward on the spiritual journey is taken in the dark, illumined only in retrospect by the light of faith.

No doubt, the great canonized saints, such as Augustine, have an inherent power to inspire and enlighten, but for us today they can seem remote, far removed from us historically, socially, and culturally. This is why Pope Francis invites us to reflect on what he calls "next-door neighbor saints" or "middle-class saints," and I am calling "unsung saints" persons who are not perfect but who keep striving for gospel ideals. The good people we encounter in our lives, who live the Christian life in simple, ordinary ways, may have a more profound affect on us than the famous followers of Christ. They can serve as examples of heeding the call to holiness and taking the next step on the spiritual journey.

An Unsung Saint

I have named my unsung saint Sue, and have somewhat disguised her story. She first came to my attention when she attended Mass at St. Thomas More University Parish in Bowling Green, Ohio, where I served as associate pastor. She came to Mass with her husband and two teenage children, and after Mass would regularly greet me with a smile and find something good to say about the homily. Over time, I got to know her and her family better and enjoyed a few home-cooked meals at her house, before which they took turns saying a short prayer thanking God for a special blessing of the day. On occasion, we had some private conversations that enabled me to learn more about her and her spiritual journey.

Early Life

Sue was the eldest of three in a Catholic family that engaged in many traditional practices: for example, attending Mass on Sunday, saying a decade of the rosary when they traveled by car, abstaining from meat on Fridays, attending Lenten devotions, participating in the rituals of Ash Wednesday and Palm Sunday, and praying to saints for specific needs.

After graduating from a public high school and faithfully attending CCD classes, Sue, in quick order, got a job, met the love of her life, got married in the church, and, within four years, gave birth to her son and daughter. She happily dedicated herself to making her marriage work and raising her children in the faith.

Family Life

Meeting these responsibilities was not always easy for her. The man she loved had a good job as a chemical engineer that demanded extra hours that cut into his family time. He was not a particularly good listener and often responded to his wife's portrayal of a demanding day with a good practical solution to her problems. He generally went to Mass with her, but much to her disappointment, shared little of his own spiritual life with her. Despite these difficulties, Sue never wavered in her love for him and used her considerable relational skills to appease him and keep the marriage intact.

As to her children, raising her son was pure joy. She loved having his friends over to the house, enjoyed watching his basketball games, was grateful that he confided in her, and felt confident that he would do well when he went away to college. She said prayers of gratitude for their satisfying relationship. Raising her daughter was much more difficult as they seemed to clash over many things, like keeping her room clean, obeying curfews, doing chores, and choosing boyfriends. It took much prayer, patience, and persevering love to survive the difficult years and eventually form a healthy adult relationship.

Spirituality

As Sue revealed more about herself, I began to sense her deep spirituality. She exuded an inner confidence based on the conviction that God loved her and a fundamental trust nourished by her early positive experiences of her Catholic faith. She manifested through her whole life an innate desire to be a good person, to do God's will, to grow in her faith. She exuded an authentic joy, arising from her consistent liturgical and private prayer life. She did not think of the heavy demands of her family life as a sacrifice or restraint but as an opportunity to share her love in a constructive, satisfying way. Grateful to God, she was proud of her efforts to be a good Christian wife and mother. That was the state of Sue's soul as I knew her in her fifties. For me, she was an unsung saint, an inspiring example of a person serious about living the Christian life and practicing the law of love on a daily basis.

Sometime in her mid-fifties, Sue attended a parish evening of reflection on the parable of the Good Samaritan. The presentation stressed the importance of practicing the command to love our neighbor, even those who are strangers or enemies. One of the points that struck her was a quote from Karl Rahner that "love is true to itself only if prepared to give more tomorrow than today."

She came home convinced that she should do more to fulfill the Lord's command to love our neighbor. She began by a weekly visit to an elderly neighbor now confined to a nursing home. This simple beginning gradually expanded as she visited her friend more often and stopped in to visit more residents. She started to feel free to pray with them and talk about spiritual joys and challenges. To enrich her encounters, she became a eucharistic minister in her parish in order to bring communion to the nursing home residents. She took her time with each person and was prepared to listen to those who wanted to talk. Over months and years, her first step grew into a dedicated ministry that brought joy and comfort to many and enriched her own personal spirituality and family life. Sue became for me an expanded version of an unsung saint. This woman who dedicated herself to forming a loving family became an example of a love that grows, that expands its scope, that looks more like the inclusive love of Christ.

As Pope Francis teaches and as the celebrated Augustine and the unsung Sue exemplify, we are all called to holiness and to make progress on our spiritual journey. At crucial points on the journey, we are challenged to discern the best next step toward a deeper love of God and neighbor. We can proceed with confidence that the Spirit will sustain all of our good efforts as we identify our excuses, pray for guidance, seek help if necessary, and take small steps forward on our journey toward greater spiritual maturity.

2

Following Our Unique Path

In his apostolic exhortation, Pope Francis insists that we find and follow our own unique path to holiness and a deeper, more robust spirituality: "The important thing is that each believer discern his or her own path, that they bring out the very best of themselves, the most personal gifts that God has placed in their hearts (cf. 1 Cor 12:7), rather than hopelessly trying to imitate something not meant for them. We are called to be witnesses, but there are many actual ways of bearing witness" (no. 11).

In this regard, it is noteworthy that the influential Jesuit theologian Karl Rahner, who wrote many beautiful prayers of his own, confessed his own misguided effort to imitate the prayer content of St. Francis of Assisi. Aware that his own piety did not spontaneously appreciate the grandeur and beauty of nature, Rahner tried to make his own the marvelous "Canticle of Creation" by Francis, praising our "Brother Son" and "Sister Moon." Unable to generate any authentic appreciation of the wonders of nature, however, Rahner concluded that we all do better following our own distinctive religious sentiments in developing our prayer life.

The hopeless, ineffective imitation identified by Pope Francis can take many forms. Lay persons who compare themselves unfavorably to celibate priests and nuns may conclude that they are not called to holiness. A couple who tried to pray together, on the advice of their pastor, found it caused more friction than good. Individuals who wanted to maintain their practice of frequent confession found that they made more spiritual progress by going less frequently but with greater meaning. Diocesan priests who tried to follow a monastic regimen of prayer could not do so due to the demands of parish ministry. A busy mother of three youngsters longed for the solitude enjoyed by her unmarried sister but was totally consumed by the demands of motherhood. There are probably cases where imitation is spiritually fruitful, but the pope's warning is well taken for most of us.

A CELEBRATED SAINT

Henri Nouwen (1932–1996), the Dutch priest and popular spiritual writer, who spent most of his adult life in the United States and Canada, serves as an instructive example of a man who struggled to find his own unique path to holiness.

Popularity

Nouwen has been an immensely popular spiritual guide for many decades. His forty books have sold over two million copies and been translated into at least twenty languages. Catholic priests ordained in the early 1980s ranked him as one of the most influential authors on their lives, along with Karl Rahner and Thomas Merton. After her husband's infidelity, Hilary Clinton said that Nouwen's book *The Return of the Prodigal Son* helped her find inner peace and to extend forgiveness. Today, he remains one of the most popular authors for individuals seeking to grow spiritually.

Henri Nouwen's enduring popularity is fascinating. He did not write a systematic theology nor did he enter into extended dialogue with the doctrinal tradition of the church. His influence flows, rather, from his personal descriptions of the broken character of human existence and from his insightful suggestions for healing those wounds.

For Nouwen, his path to holiness was clearly connected to his personal struggle with an acute sense of loneliness. In his bestselling book *The Wounded Healer*, he wrote:

> We live in a society in which loneliness has become one of the most painful human wounds. The growing competition and rivalry that pervade our lives from birth have created within us an acute awareness of our isolation. This awareness has in turn left many with a heightened anxiety and an intense search for the experience of unity and community. It has also led people to ask anew how love, friendship, brotherhood and sisterhood can free us from isolation and offer us a sense of intimacy and belonging.

Growing up, Henri always felt loved by his mother, but believed that he could never do enough to earn the love of his success-oriented father. After his ordination in 1957, he chose to do graduate studies in psychology rather than theology, enabling him to probe more deeply his own inner struggles. During his almost two decades in the academic world, teaching at Notre Dame, Yale, and Harvard, he never really felt at home. The great acclaim he received from his books and lectures never fully satisfied him but left him with feelings of inadequacy and low self-esteem. Near the end of his years at Harvard, he found himself in "a very dark place," isolated from other people and feeling "spiritually dead."

Nouwen was convinced that his struggles with loneliness could help others deal with their own brokenness. In his vast writings, we find many valuable gospel-inspired suggestions for spiritual healing. Let us reflect on two especially relevant ones.

Trapeze Act

From an early age, Henri was fascinated by the trapeze acts that he saw at the circus. As an adult, he got to know the Flying Rodleighs, a South African trapeze troupe. They allowed him to travel with them and, on occasion, to swing on the trapeze and fall into the net, where he would jump around with great glee. He appreciated the strict discipline of the Rodleighs, as well as their sense of community and their physical skills. They became his "tutors in theology" and spiritual guides, who reminded him of the importance of living in the present moment. Nouwen came to see that the real star of the act was not the flyer, who soars through the air, but the catcher, who extends his hands ready to receive and welcome the flyer. For Nouwen, the trapeze act served as a metaphor for the spiritual life. The key to spiritual growth is to trust God, who always extends open arms to catch us. With his usual candor, Nouwen once admitted that he "had lived most of my life as a tightrope artist trying to walk on a high, thin cable from one tower to the other, always waiting for the applause." Tutored by the Rodleighs, Nouwen invites us to embrace our brokenness, with trust in the "divine Catcher," who is always ready to save us.

The Prodigal Son

In 1983, Nouwen just happened to see a print of Rembrandt's famous painting "The Return of the Prodigal Son." He was immediately fascinated by it, especially the embrace between father and son, which touched his own deep longings for acceptance. In 1986, he traveled to the Hermitage in Saint Petersburg, Russia, and spent hours prayerfully gazing at the actual painting, which came to represent for him the entire gospel. He had spent his academic career trying to get a glimpse of God by analyzing human experience from the perspective of the gospel. In contemplating the painting, he was touched at a more emotional level, drawn into an interior place where he could be embraced by an all-loving Father who offers a joy and peace not of this world. Nouwen identified himself with the prodigal son, who left his father's house and went to a foreign land. He saw himself repeating this destructive pattern by inordinately seeking achievement and acclaim. He recognized his loneliness as a sign that he had left home and forgotten that he is the beloved son of the Father. In the painting, the father's embrace of his wayward son is strong and comforting, welcoming and forgiving. With such deep love, there is no need for explanation or apology. Inspired by Rembrandt's portrayal of the familiar gospel story, Nouwen reminds all of us that we are beloved of the Father, who welcomes us home.

Gustavo Gutiérrez

In the early 1980s, Nouwen continued his spiritual quest by spending time in Latin America, living with the poor for months and learning from Gustavo Gutiérrez, the father of liberation theology. Nouwen came to see that his own spirituality was "excessively spiritualized, individualistic, interior, elitist and romantic." He dreamed of founding a community of committed persons who would serve the poor by living with them. Eventually, he came to see that this spiritual path would not work for him because of his great need for emotional support and because the struggle for justice often left him discouraged and disheartened.

Daybreak

In his ongoing search for a viable spiritual path, in 1985, Nouwen went to live in the L'Arche Daybreak community near Toronto to serve the mentally challenged residents, who form the core of the community. He was assigned to care for Adam Arnett, who was unable to talk or care for himself. Over time, Nouwen became more comfortable with Adam, patiently getting him up in the morning, bathing, dressing, shaving, and feeding him. When Adam died at the age of thirty-four, Henri preached at his funeral, calling Adam "his counselor, teacher and guide, who could never say a word to me but taught me more than anyone else." He added, Adam "called me home," "home in my own body" and "home in the body of the church" and concluded that without Adam, "I would not know where I would be today." Not everything went smoothly for Nouwen while at Daybreak. Early in his years there, he fell in love with a man who did not reciprocate his feelings, which sent Henri into a severe depression that dissipated only after months of intense therapy, supported by good friends. Nevertheless, we can say that this talented man found his path to holiness and a degree of inner peace not in a highly successful academic career or in writing influential books, but in a life of service, caring for one of God's most vulnerable individuals.

Henri Nouwen serves as an especially instructive example of finding and following our own path to holiness for various reasons: he revealed his own struggles in finding a viable path; he kept searching despite false starts; he continued to rely on God's help and guidance; and he found a path forward in unlikely circumstances, reminding us that our God works in mysterious ways.

AN UNSUNG SAINT

I will call my unsung saint "Bill" and will disguise his story. Bill was born into an affluent, nominally Catholic family, the first of two sons. At his mother's initiative, he was baptized and made his First Communion, but after that seldom went to Mass and received very little formal religious education. His father was the dominant influence in the family, a college football player and a very successful corporate executive, a hard-driving, no-nonsense man who put his job above his family. Growing up, Bill idolized his father and was determined to win his approval. Working hard, he got good grades in school and played high school football, which pleased his father.

With some family help, he got accepted into the same elite business school that his father attended. Again, he studied diligently and got good grades but was not big enough to play football at the collegiate level. The thought of going to church on campus never entered his mind, although he did go to midnight Mass on Christmas when home with his parents and younger brother. Periodically, he dated some women friends, but nothing serious developed. Earning a degree in business administration was a happy accomplishment for Bill, especially since his father joined his mother in congratulating him warmly. At his father's urging, Bill went on to get a master's degree in finance, which helped him get a good job with a well-known brokerage firm. Showing some of the same drive as his father, Bill worked his way up the corporate ladder, and in twelve years became a junior vice president. At this point, he was in his late thirties, with his dream job, a sizeable income, and the approval of his father; but he realized he was not happy. Paradoxically, his career success left him unsettled, conflicted, and dissatisfied.

Meeting Emily

At this troubled point in his life, Bill met Emily, a devout Catholic about his age, unmarried, happily employed as a registered nurse in a local hospital. It was not love at first sight, but he found himself fascinated by her simple lifestyle and serene outlook so different from his own driven, competitive approach. From the beginning, he felt she knew something about life that he didn't and was determined to learn more about it. They dated, talked seriously, and started going to Mass together. It became clear to him that Emily was different from his other female friends: she liked going to church; she talked openly about God and her faith; she prayed a lot; she got enjoyment out of simple things; she did not need to win an argument; she was content with her job; and she radiated an inner peace and joy. When he told Emily he was in love with her, he was amazed and thrilled that she shared his feelings. He also knew that he wanted her not just to be his lover but his mentor, who would help him gain the serenity she had. To do this, he was going to have to quit his job, get out of the competitive rat race that had always dominated his life. Telling his father was the most difficult part of the process. It did not go well. His father thought he was crazy to leave a position that he had worked so hard to achieve and that had such potential for further advancement.

Growing Spiritually

In getting married, Bill committed himself to being a good partner to Emily, which meant for him becoming a better Catholic with an authentic spirituality. His pastor, who gave good homilies, was especially helpful in recommending spiritual books for him to read. His initial efforts centered on understanding the Mass better and participating more actively. The idea of seeing the Eucharist as a gift exchange appealed to him, so at Mass he got in the habit of offering his efforts to grow spiritually to God through Christ and receiving communion as a nourishing gift from God. An article on prayer helped him realize that he had to find, with God's help, his own best way of praying and not try to imitate what Emily did. Over time, he found that it worked best if he spent about fifteen minutes at the beginning of his day and at the end talking to God in his own words, expressing gratitude for Emily and asking God to bless their marriage.

Influence of Merton

Thanks to a suggestion from his pastor, Bill became a big fan of the Trappist monk Thomas Merton. He saw something of himself in Merton's story of his conversion to Catholicism from a very secular way of life, recounted in *The Seven Storey Mountain*. Merton's ongoing quest for inner peace reminded him of his own search for the kind of serenity that first attracted him to Emily. Merton's notion that to try to pray is already an authentic act of prayer gave him hope that his struggling efforts were valuable in themselves. The Trappist monk's lyrical praise of leisure, silence, and doing nothing suggested he had to learn to balance work and leisure in his own life. Merton's book *Conjectures of a Guilty Bystander* made Bill reflect on how little he had done to help others when he had a lot of money, and how he had to find new ways to contribute to charity and work for justice. The monk's striking prayer that starts "My Lord God, I have no idea where I am going. I do not see the road ahead of me . . . nor do I really know myself" somehow comforted Bill and helped him accept his limited efforts to become a more spiritual person. Merton also taught him that directly seeking serenity would prove to be elusive, and that he would find genuine peace only as a by-product of trying to do God's will. Finally, Merton convinced him not to compare his spiritual journey with the journey of anyone else, including his wife.

Bill has continued his efforts to grow spiritually by actively participating in the life of his parish: functioning as a lector at Mass, which moves him to pay better attention to the Liturgy of the Word; serving on the parish finance council, which taps the skills developed in his previous life; contributing 5 percent of his more modest income, as a business manager for a local nonprofit, to the church, which is part of his effort to become a more generous person; and giving presentations with Emily in the marriage preparation program, which stimulates honest private conversation with her on the state of their own marriage. He is also looking for ways to participate in the parish justice and peace programs so that he does not end up as a "guilty bystander."

Application

Bill's story reminds us that it might not be easy to find our own unique path to holiness and that we should be open to making adjustments on our journey. Excessive efforts to please and impress others can lead us down paths to dissatisfaction and emptiness. Comparing our spiritual growth to others is dangerous since it is likely to lead to either pride or envy. It is only by staying open to the guidance of the Holy Spirit that we can keep a steady course on our unique path to greater spiritual maturity.

3

Ordinary Life as a Path to Holiness

The path to holiness passes through our everyday lives and ordinary activities. Most of us grow spiritually not by spectacular deeds but by meeting our daily responsibilities and finding deeper meaning in all we do. In his exhortation, Pope Francis makes this point in various ways. We "grow in holiness by responsibly and generously carrying out our proper mission" (no. 24). "This holiness to which the Lord calls you will grow through small gestures" (no. 16). "Every moment can be an expression of self-sacrificing love," and "every minute of our lives can be a step along the path to growth in holiness" (no. 31).

The teaching that ordinary life provides the path to holiness may not be immediately evident and is clearly difficult to practice. Life, with all its demands and distractions, can seem more like an obstacle course than a path to spiritual maturity. It is possible to sleepwalk through the routines of everyday life, oblivious to their spiritual significance. We can be paralyzed by the false assumption that long hours in prayer are the only way to holiness and by the illusion that one of these days we will be less busy and harried so that we can attend to spiritual matters.

Pope Francis recognizes that "new gadgets" and "an endless array of consumer goods" can overwhelm us and drown out God's voice. His solution, however, is not to withdraw from the world or give up on holiness but to live a balanced life as "contemplative even in the midst of action" (no. 26). We need times when we halt the "rat race" and "recover the personal space needed to carry on a heartfelt dialogue with God" (no. 29). The pope reminds us that the daily routine that serves as our path to holiness must include not only family and work responsibilities but also prayer and reflection. A balanced life of praying to God and loving our neighbor creates a more reliable path to spiritual growth.

A CELEBRATED SAINT

Saint Thérèse of Lisieux (1873–1897), commonly known as the "Little Flower," serves as a classic model of using daily activities as the path to sanctity. Thérèse Martin, the youngest of five sisters, entered the Carmelite convent in Lisieux at the age of fifteen and died of tuberculosis before she reached her twenty-fifth birthday. She did not attend a university, get a degree in theology, or write scholarly books. Nevertheless, in 1997, just a century after her death, Pope John Paul II declared her a Doctor of the Universal Church. She joined a select list of thirty-three persons, including the eminent scholars Augustine and Aquinas, and two other women, Teresa of Avila and Catherine of Siena. Doctors of the Church are chosen because their teachings conform to revealed truth and shed new light on the mysteries of the faith. The pope noted that Thérèse, although the youngest of all the doctors, showed such maturity in the spiritual journey that her profound insights merit her "a place among the great spiritual masters." Her spirituality centered on charity, which she saw as the essence of the Christian life and the key to her own vocation. According to her testimony, the Lord himself taught her "the lesson of love," which is "the secret of perfection" often denied to scholars.

The focus on charity is made explicit in her autobiography, *Story of a Soul*, one of the most popular spiritual books of the twentieth century. The text consists of three manuscripts that she wrote at different times in response to commands from her superiors. She was a woman of tremendous passion and high ideals, who from her youth felt destined to greatness. She felt called to be "a fighter, a priest, an apostle, a doctor, a martyr" and to perform "every kind of heroic action at once," all for the love of God. Her passion was to travel all over the world, "preaching the gospel on all five continents and in the most distant lands, all at once." She longed to be a heroic martyr like Joan of Arc.

Everyday Charity

Living a simple life of prayer in a convent, Thérèse felt tormented by these burning ambitions and "unfulfilled longings." Amid her frustration, she turned to Paul's First Letter to the Corinthians, which reminded her that not everyone can be an apostle or a prophet but that all members of the Body of Christ have their own role to play in the church. She recognized the truth in these verses, but they did not set her heart at rest. Reading further in the text, she came to the lines: "Prize the best gifts of heaven. Meanwhile, I can show you a way which is better than any other." The great Pauline insight that charity is the best way of all brought her a great sense of peace. Charity was the "key to her vocation." Love is "the vocation which includes all others." She had found her niche. "To be nothing else than love" is to be "everything at once." She had discovered a way to satisfy her immense passion and fulfill her great dreams through the little way of everyday charity. With this insight, a restful calm came over her as she saw "the beacon of love," like a lighthouse, guiding her. She understood her vocation as a call to live the law of love in the ordinary circumstances of her convent life. "Love is all the skill I have," she wrote, recognizing that her task was not to be a great missionary but "to do the tiniest things right" for the sake of charity. She wanted to seize every opportunity to love others, including simple gestures such as a smile or a kind word. Her redirected passion resonated with the conviction of John of the Cross: "the

slightest movement of disinterested love has more value
than all the other acts of a human soul put together."

Prayer

Thérèse understood the importance of prayer in living the
life of charity. For her, it was always better to talk to God
than to talk about God. She prayed to Jesus, her "first
and only love," to help her in her weakness and fragility
to remain faithful to the path of self-sacrificing love. Even
when she experienced no consolation in her prayers and
activities, she counted on her Beloved to lend her eagle
wings so that she could still soar toward the "Sun of Love."
Her deepest hope was that the Divine Word, who loved
her fondly, would one day carry her to "the very center of
love" and consume her in "love's furnace."

Examples

In her autobiography, Thérèse recorded examples of her
little way of practicing charity in ordinary situations.
Recalling that Jesus identified himself with the most insig-
nificant individuals, she swallowed her pride and went out
of her way to help a very demanding crippled sister get
from the chapel to the refectory. She tried to carry out
this daily routine with the utmost care and compassion:
walking the sister at the proper pace, helping her sit down
without causing pain, cutting her food, and always giving
her a big smile at the end of this daily ritual.

At times, the little way of charity called for creative ways of managing her negative inclinations. At evening prayer, she sat in front of a sister who continually made an annoying sound like rubbing two shells together. Thérèse longed to turn around and give her a disapproving look. But something "deep down inside her" told her she should put up with it for the love of God and spare the sister any embarrassment. She attempted to ignore the sound and block it out of her mind, but this just increased her agitation and caused greater distraction in her prayer. Her next strategy was more creative: she tried to like the irritating noise, hearing it as a delightful sound and offering this music to God in prayer. It worked remarkably well. The little way of charity transformed an irritant into prayer.

Application

Thérèse is a helpful spiritual guide with an important contemporary message. She calls us to simplify our daily activities and to find deeper meaning in the ordinary routines of life. Her little way of charity is rooted in solid theological insights. We are totally dependent on God, who loves us. We are blessed with a loving personal relationship with Christ, who calls us to live his law of love in all aspects of our lives, including the most ordinary activities. Thérèse's theological base is quite narrow, but it is solid. Her writing is subjective and personal, but it contains a universal message. Her spiritual insights are limited but resonate with many people today. She is a safe guide because her advice flows from her healthy theological sensibilities. According to Pope John Paul II, it is the "convergence of doctrine and concrete experience" in the life of Thérèse that makes her "an attractive model" for people today seeking a deeper meaning in life. The "disarming simplicity" of her "little way" encourages us to return to the essential gospel imperative of love, which is at the center of Christian discipleship.

Focus on Charity

More specifically, Thérèse suggests that the key to managing complexity is an interior focus on the fundamental virtue of charity. A proper love of self, which accepts the essential limitations of life, enables us to deal better with our confusing emotions, including the frustration of failed ideals. Love of neighbor guides and motivates our efforts to clarify and heal troublesome relationships. Finally, love of God encourages us to do our part in the complicated struggle for justice and peace, while leaving the outcome in the hands of the Compassionate One. The little way of Thérèse of Lisieux, rooted in charity, reminds all of us that the path to sanctity passes through everyday life and ordinary activities.

AN UNSUNG SAINT

Most of us can identify someone we know who has inspired us by the way they have lived their Christian faith on a daily basis. I will call my own unsung saint "G. L." as I highlight his everyday virtues without claiming an exaggerated perfection. G. L., who was born in the United States, grew up in a large, poor, devout Catholic family (two of his older sisters were nuns) of Czech immigrants on a farm near Pittsburgh. He was ambitious and hard-working and developed a passion for baseball and, later, other sports. He was the first male in his family to go to college, attending Duquesne University, where, as a freshman, he was the starting catcher on the baseball team. As a youth living at home, he courageously confronted his abusive father and put an end to his harsh treatment of his mother. Deeply affected by his mother's sufferings, he vowed never to abuse others, a promise he kept in raising his own family, never even spanking his children, as was then customary. In his everyday life, he insisted that problems be solved not by harsh language or sullen pouting but by civil discussion and reasonable compromise. By breaking the cycle of abuse, he made a truly significant, if generally unrecognized, contribution to the good of his family and future generations.

Employment

The need to support himself and his parents forced G. L. to cut short his academic and baseball career and to take a job with the Great Atlantic and Pacific Tea Company, which brought him to Toledo. Here he ran the coffee plant, met and married the love of his life, and raised his family. He was dedicated to doing a good job managing the plant, working long hours to get the operation started and keeping it running efficiently for over thirty years. He demanded good work from the fifteen or so employees, but was attentive to their individual needs. He used his managerial position to do good for others. Every week, he had a large package of free coffee set aside for the Little Sisters of the Poor and their ministry to the elderly. He brought two of his unemployed brothers-in-law from Pittsburgh to work in the plant so they could support their families. Part of his effort to create a healthy work environment was to make sure the female workers were respected by the men.

Husband

As a husband, G. L. did not rise much above the patriarchal patterns of the day, and early in his marriage pushed a well-intentioned, but disruptive and short-lived, move to bring his mother into their home. Nevertheless, he did exercise virtue in his married life: making decisions typically intended to please his wife; always treating her with respect and never speaking harshly; being especially attentive when she was not feeling well or was overburdened; doing fun things together, like enjoying picnics and athletic events; and becoming, over their forty-four years of marriage, somewhat more dialogic and collaborative.

Father

As a father, he instructed his children in the ways of the Catholic faith, mostly by his good example. During much of his later adult life, even when working long hours, he often attended daily Mass, highlighting the centrality of the Eucharist in Catholic spirituality. His personal prayer centered on gratitude for his many blessings and petitions for his family and friends, suggesting a mature approach to prayer. In preparing the household budget, he began by setting aside money for the parish collection and for a number of charities, indicating proper Christian priorities.

Catholic Faith

His understanding of his Catholic tradition was open, generous, and inclusive. He and his wife befriended a Jewish couple down the block, suggesting the value of Catholic–Jewish dialogue. When some Catholics spoke negatively about a Protestant minister living in the neighborhood, he defended him as a good Christian man, anticipating the ecumenism promoted by Vatican II. In fact, he seldom spoke negatively of any person, including his own father and individuals who angered him, exemplifying an important gospel mandate. When individuals made mistakes, even big ones, he typically supported forgiveness and second chances, giving witness to a central teaching of Jesus. Without naming it, he practiced to a high degree the virtue of *epikeia*, which enables one to know when and how to break the rules, implicitly indicating that the Catholic religion could not be reduced to keeping a series of laws.

I am deeply grateful to my father, George L. Bacik, for so many things: for serving as my prime example of using everyday life as the path to holiness; for heroically breaking the cycle of domestic abuse so his family could enjoy a peaceful life; for sharing with me his great appreciation for my mother and her marvelous qualities (for example, "Your mother is amazing at managing money," and, when I was about twelve, "Your mother looks as good to me today as the day I married her"); for modeling healthy role adaptations (for example, as an older parent, he asked my advice on how to deal with my much younger teenage sister growing up in a rapidly changing world); for teaching me a broad, open version of Catholicism that enabled me to survive the narrow legalism of my seminary education; and for encouraging me to look for the unique goodness of each person, which I have at least tried to do throughout my priestly ministry. My father, George L. Bacik, is an unsung saint, a man who reminds all of us that everyday life is filled with opportunities for spiritual growth.

4

Imitating Christ

For Christians, the path to holiness is marked out by Jesus Christ and his example of faithful obedience to God's will and dedicated service to spreading the divine reign in the world. The Christian life is empowered and guided by the example of the historical Jesus and the mediation of the risen Christ. We grow spiritually by deepening our personal relationship to Christ and strengthening our commitment to follow his teachings. In the exhortation, Pope Francis emphasizes the centrality of our relationship to Christ: "At its core, holiness is experiencing, in union with Christ, the mysteries of his life. It consists in uniting ourselves to the Lord's death and resurrection in a unique and personal way, constantly dying and rising anew with him" (no. 20). According to the pope, an integrated Christian spirituality has a paschal character in that it includes participation in both the death and the resurrection of Christ. Our path to holiness is marked by liturgical celebrations of both Good Friday and Easter Sunday, which unite us with the crucified and risen Christ. Daily, we have opportunities to die and rise with Christ by following his command to love our neighbor.

Francis also encourages us to reproduce in our own lives "various aspects of Jesus's earthly life: his hidden life, his life in community, his closeness to the outcast, his poverty and other ways in which he showed his self-sacrificing love" (no. 20). The pope wants us to reflect on the historical Jesus portrayed in the Gospels and to follow his example in our daily lives. We are called to put on the mind of Christ so that we see the world through the eyes of faith illumined by him and are committed to practice his command to love our neighbor. Jesus Christ is our path to holiness and our way to greater spiritual maturity.

A CELEBRATED SAINT

The German Jesuit theologian Karl Rahner (1904–1984) serves as an example of an intellectually solid and personally integrated spirituality centered on the historical Jesus and risen Christ. Karl was born March 5, 1904, in Freiburg, the middle child of seven in a devout Catholic family. He joined the Society of Jesus in 1922 and was ordained in 1932; studied at various universities, including Freiburg, where he encountered the philosopher Martin Heidegger; spent his life teaching, lecturing, and writing in an effort to make the Catholic tradition relevant for contemporary life; served as an influential theological consultant at the Second Vatican Council; and continued to write on current issues until shortly before his death in 1984.

First Meeting

It was in 1974 that I first met Karl Rahner at his Jesuit residence in Munich, Germany. I was planning to work on a dissertation on Rahner at Oxford University and wanted to get to know him personally. When I told him I wanted to write something on his theology, he replied that such things are as the sands of the seashore, adding that he did not have long to talk with me. Despite this rocky start, I sensed that we would get along. My intuition proved correct, as we engaged in a long, stimulating conversation during which he shared some off-the-record opinions of other theologians and proudly showed me a draft of what would become his masterwork, *Foundations of Christian Faith*. After an hour-and-twenty-minute wide-ranging conversation, I thanked him for his time, and then this short, pudgy, volatile, energetic, chain-smoking, theological giant got up, put his arm around me and asked that I pray for his happy death. I left this encounter not sure exactly how to interpret this request but with increased confidence that studying Rahner's theology in greater depth was a potentially fruitful project.

Interactions

In 1976, while I was writing my dissertation at Oxford, I spent some months in Munich, with periodic opportunities to interact with Rahner, a leisurely walk, some serious conversations, and shared meals. I spent my days in the

library reading some of his unpublished class notes, filled
with biblical citations and quotes from the church fathers
and medieval theologians, much more background material than found in his published works. On one occasion,
he asked me to read and critique a dissertation on his
thought by an English-speaking American theologian.
Later I found out that he shared my evaluation with the
author, just as I had written it. On Holy Thursday, I
attended Mass in the chapel with a small group of Jesuits
living in the house. Sitting in the front row dressed in suit
and tie, Rahner went to the ambo after the reading of the
Gospel about the washing of feet and read a thoughtful
homily that stressed, among other things, the importance
of seeing the organic connection between Christ's presence at the Last Supper and his presence in the eucharistic
meal and in everyday life. His homily, carefully prepared
for a small group of friends, was a good example of his
ability to relate Gospel teachings to real life.

A Last Meeting

The last time I saw Rahner was in December 1977, when
he wrote an introduction for the published version of my
dissertation, *Apologetics and the Eclipse of Mystery: Mystagogy according to Karl Rahner.* He started out by trying to
dictate it in English to a seminarian struggling to type it
correctly. It went better after I convinced Rahner to dictate it in German, which we could translate later. It was
quite an experience for me watching this energetic man

pace the floor and dictate those typically long complex sentences. After he was finished, I told him that his statement about not taking many criticisms seriously sounded arrogant, but he replied sternly that he stood by his statement and would not change it.

His Advice

When I departed from Munich in December 1977, I left a note for Rahner thanking him for enabling me to remain a Catholic priest with intellectual honesty and for showing me how to draw on the Christian tradition to promote spiritual growth. In my pastoral ministry, I have tried to remember his sage advice: do not become my disciple but try to make the gospel relevant in your own setting.

Christology

Karl Rahner wrote extensively on the major issues in Christology and penned numerous meditations on the earthly Jesus. On the much-debated question of the relationship between the historical Jesus and the Christ of faith, Rahner wanted to avoid basing faith on particular Gospel passages that may be shown to be unreliable by Scripture scholars. Although he was convinced that the New Testament gives us a substantially correct picture of the historical Jesus, he preferred to base Christian faith in Christ on the indisputable fact that Jesus claimed to be the absolute Savior and that his disciples came to accept that claim.

The New Testament expresses this decisive centrality of Christ in various ways. The Letter to the Colossians proclaims the cosmic significance of Christ as "the image of the invisible God, the firstborn of all creation." Every created reality, visible and invisible, was created "through him and for him." Absolute fullness resides in him, and primacy is his in everything. Christ reconciles everything on earth and in the heavens in his person (see 1:15–20). The Gospel of Luke presents Christ as the center point of history, a more significant figure than the Roman emperor, Caesar Augustus. In Mark's Gospel, Christ appears as the surpassing exorcist with power over Satan and all the demons. John's Gospel exalts Jesus as the Son of God, the Word made flesh, who makes striking claims: "The Father and I are one" (John 10:30) and "I am the way and the truth and the life" (John 14:6). Rahner's argument is based not on the historical reliability of any particular scriptural verse but on the cumulative witness of the whole New Testament to the claim that Jesus is the absolute Savior and the definitive Prophet.

For Rahner, much of the popular understanding of the Incarnation seems mythological, something like a Hindu avatar who comes down to earth, intervenes briefly in human affairs, and then returns to heaven. To counter this danger, he developed what he calls "a transcendental Christology," which presents the Incarnation as an intrinsic possibility within a material evolving world, which has God as its intrinsic dynamism and final goal.

Rahner describes the material world as "frozen spirit" with an innate potential of developing toward more complex forms, which eventually produced human beings, who are inspirited bodies or enfleshed spirits capable of thinking and loving. With the arrival of human beings, the evolving world became conscious of itself. As human history progressed, some human beings became more open, more receptive to God's self-giving. During what the German philosopher Karl Jaspers called the "Axial Age," about 800 to 200 BC, especially receptive human beings appeared in various parts of the world: Confucius in China; Siddhartha Gautama, the Buddha, in India; Isaiah in Israel; and Socrates in Greece. Mindful of this historical development, Rahner says that we can imagine a point where God's self-giving and human reception would meet in a person who is totally open to divine love. This person would be God Incarnate in the world. The Christian claim is that this potential high point in the dialogue between God and the human family did actually occur in history, in the person of Jesus of Nazareth. From this perspective, the Incarnation does not appear as mythological but as the fulfillment of an evolving historical process that makes God's loving plan to save all people definitive and irrevocable. The historical interaction between God and the human family, always a mix of sin and more powerful grace, continues into the unknown future; but as Rahner put it, "The seeds of the final victory are already planted."

In discussing the resurrection of Christ, Rahner reminds us that it is not the resuscitation of his body but rather the validity of his life and message and the vindication of his claim to be the absolute Savior. As Christians, we follow the Lord, who is both crucified and risen; we profess belief in both his death and his resurrection and celebrate liturgically both Good Friday and Easter Sunday. The resurrection enables us to believe what we desperately hope is true, that none of our efforts to do good are ever wasted and that all of our virtuous actions have permanent validity. Belief in the resurrection encompasses important truths: God is trustworthy and faithful to the divine promises; Christ is Savior of all as he claimed; the Holy Spirit lives within us as Christ promised; death is not the end but leads to new life; divine grace is more powerful than human sin; love is our most valuable renewable resource; and the final victory of good over evil is guaranteed. Following Rahner's line of thought, we can think of the resurrection as a second Big Bang, releasing an inexhaustible spiritual energy into the world that sustains not just Christian believers but all people of good will.

The Humanity of Christ

Rahner was convinced that many Christians have trouble identifying with Christ because they do not really accept his true humanity. They have a strong belief in the divinity of Christ, who is "true God from true God, begotten, not made, consubstantial with the Father," as we proclaim in the Nicene Creed. However, they have more difficulty accepting that Jesus experienced genuine human reactions; for example, that he had conflicts with his parents, got angry, knew disappointment, wept over the death of a friend, did not know when the end of the world was coming; and felt abandoned by God.

Traditional theology, based on John's Gospel, started with the conviction that the eternal Word of God descended from heaven to become man and save us from our sins. It went on to portray Jesus as the exalted Son of God, the creator of all things, and the source of truth—images that highlight the divinity of Christ. To gain a more balanced outlook, Rahner developed an ascending Christology that begins with the human Jesus portrayed in the Synoptic Gospels, who grew in wisdom, age, and grace before God and man. For Rahner, Jesus was so open to God, so obedient to the Father's will, and so filled with divine grace that we can confess him as Son of God, God personally present in our world, the definitive Prophet and absolute Savior, the fullness of divine revelation. As true man and true God, Jesus Christ is our model of holiness and our guide to spiritual maturity. We can identify with him as our brother and friend because he was like us in all things but sin. We can have a personal relationship with him because, as the risen Lord, he remains present to us in all our everyday activities, in our liturgical celebrations, and in the needy we encounter.

Gospel Studies

Not only did Rahner encourage us to imitate Christ, he also gave many concrete examples of how the Gospel stories of Jesus can guide our spiritual quest. For example, the multiplication of the loaves and fishes, told six times in the Gospels, teaches us to put an emphasis not on what we do not have, as did the disciples in the story, but on what we do have, as did Jesus, who made good use of limited resources. The story of the twelve-year-old Jesus remaining behind in the Jerusalem Temple reminds us that conflicts are inevitable in family life and that they can occur without anyone actually being at fault, as was the case with the holy family. As these examples suggest, the Gospel stories are a rich resource for finding our way on the path to holiness. Christ is present in the proclamation of the Gospel at Mass with a personal message of enlightenment and encouragement for each of us. Private prayer prepares us to take those liturgical messages to heart so they can illumine and energize our spiritual journey.

Loving Christ

As a dedicated Jesuit, Rahner's own spirituality was grounded in the *Spiritual Exercises* of St. Ignatius, which invites imaginative meditation on Gospel scenes. A chronological examination of Rahner's vast writings suggests that over time his own spirituality became more heartfelt, more emotional, and more centered on a loving, personal relationship with Christ. As a young man, he spoke rather soberly about his commitment to Christ. It was only later in life, as he himself tells it, that he could speak comfortably about "throwing his arms around Jesus in an act of love." The very fact that a great theologian continued to grow in his relationship with Christ encourages us to look for ways to deepen our own dedication to the Lord who promises us a more abundant life.

A Prayer

Consider this prayer found in Rahner's marvelous collection *Encounters with Silence*:

> Grant, O Infinite God, that I may ever cling
>   fast to Jesus Christ, my Lord.
> Let his heart reveal to me how You are disposed
>   toward me.
> I shall look upon his heart when I desire to
>   know Who You are.
> But I have still one more request.
> Make my heart like that of Your son.
> Make it as great and rich in love as His,
> so that my brothers and sisters—or at least
>   some of them,
> sometime in my life—can enter through this
>   door
> and there learn that You love him.
> God of Our Lord Jesus Christ, let me find You
>   in his heart.

An Unsung Saint

As Pope Francis reminds us, we can find inspiration not only from well-known persons but also from holy people who do not gain much public recognition. June grew up in a loving Catholic family, went to parochial schools, and married a man she met in the Newman Club in college. She liked being a mother to her four children and is proud of them, although disappointed that two of them no longer go to church. Now in her early sixties, she continues to enjoy time with her grandchildren and her challenging job with an advertising agency.

For most of her adult life, June practiced a traditional form of devotional Catholicism. She went to Mass regularly, highlighted by receiving Christ her God in communion. She had a deep devotion to Mary and said at least a decade of the rosary most days. She thought of Mary as her guide to living the Christian life, turning to her in challenging times. For example, when she was upset with her husband, fatigued with the demands of motherhood, or frustrated with her job, praying to Mary brought her a degree of comfort, believing that a saintly woman who understood her problems was with her in the struggle. When June's younger brother died at an early age, she found solace in imagining Mary holding her crucified son in her arms.

When June was in her mid-fifties, she attended a lecture sponsored by her parish on Jesus, our brother and friend, which presented in a popular form Karl Rahner's ideas on appreciating the humanity of Christ and following his example portrayed in the Gospels. It proved to be the beginning of a process that has gradually enriched her spirituality. While maintaining her devotion to Mary, she now sees Christ as her primary guide to holiness. Without being able to articulate it clearly, she has an intuitive sense that Christ understands her struggles and walks with her on her spiritual journey. She sees him as a close friend who is always there for her. She is now in the habit of listening carefully to the Gospels proclaimed at Mass, looking for a message she can apply to her everyday life. In her private prayers, she talks to Jesus in her own words, thanking him for blessings, praising him for his goodness, and asking him to forgive her sins.

As we try to deepen and expand our own relationship to Christ, it is helpful to find images and language that fit our personality and stage of spiritual development. Some of us may not be comfortable with Rahner's notion of throwing our arms around Jesus as a loving gesture or June's language of intimate friendship. There are many other constructive ways of imaging Christ: for example, the ethical teacher, who keeps us heading in the right direction; the definitive Prophet, who speaks God's word to us; the absolute Savior, who forgives our sins and always gives us another chance; the liberator of captives, who encourages us to work for justice and peace; and the cosmic Lord, who invites us to care for own common home.

It is crucial for our spiritual growth to deepen our personal relationship with Christ. This enables us to see him as the supreme model of holiness and the primary guide on our spiritual journey. It also prompts us to pray to him in words that are familiar and authentic.

5

Working for Justice

Authentic Christian holiness embraces the commitment to work for justice in our world. In the exhortation, Pope Francis states clearly: "We cannot hold up an ideal of holiness that would ignore injustice in a world where some revel, spend with abandon, and live only for the latest consumer goods, even as others look on from afar, living their entire lives in abject poverty" (no. 101). The great Hebrew prophets placed the pursuit of justice at the center of their message. Isaiah, for instance, insisted, "Seek justice, rescue the oppressed, defend the orphan, plead for the widow" (Isa 1:17). Later in the Book of Isaiah, we are told that what pleases God is "to share your bread with the hungry and bring the homeless poor into your house" (Isa 58:7–8). In his Sermon on the Mount, Jesus, continuing the prophetic tradition, teaches, "Blessed are those who hunger and thirst for righteousness, for they will be filled" (Matt 5:6). Francis insists that we express our intense desire for righteousness by pursuing justice for the most vulnerable, the poor and the weak, "even if we may not always see the fruit of our efforts" (no. 77). In pursuing justice for all, the pope advocates following the consistent ethic of life by protecting the innocent unborn as well as the poor, the abandoned, the destitute, the underprivileged, and the victims of new forms of slavery (no. 101). Commitment to the cause of justice is an essential component of our vocation to holiness and our quest for greater spiritual maturity.

A Celebrated Saint

In his 2015 address to the U.S. Congress, Pope Francis raised up the example of Dr. Martin Luther King Jr., who led the march from Selma to Montgomery in 1965. He praised King for inspiring us with his dream of "full civil and political rights," which leads to "action, participation and commitment" and which awakens what is "deepest and truest in the life of a people."

Studies

Dr. King does indeed serve as a prime example of the commitment to justice that is at the core of Christian practice. Martin was born January 15, 1929, and named for his father, the pastor of the Ebenezer Baptist Church in Atlanta, Georgia. From a young age, he was immersed in the life of the church, which proved to be vitally influential on his life. When he was a high school student, he traveled by bus to a debate contest in Dublin, Georgia, and on the return trip was forced to give up his seat to a white person—a humiliating experience that produced in him a deep anger. A good student, he entered Morehouse College in Atlanta at age fifteen; attended Crozier Seminary in Chester, Pennsylvania, from 1948 to 1951; and completed his doctorate in theology at Boston University four years later with a dissertation comparing the theology of God in the Lutheran theologian Paul Tillich and the Unitarian philosopher Henry Nelson Wieman.

Bus Boycott

In May 1954, King made the crucial decision to pursue a career as a pastor rather than a professor of theology, taking a position as pastor of the Dexter Avenue Baptist Church in Montgomery, Alabama. Within a year, he was deeply involved in the Montgomery Bus Boycott, occasioned by the arrest of Rosa Parks for refusing to give up her seat to a white person. During that long, bitter struggle against racist customs, Martin was viciously attacked, and even his house was firebombed. On one occasion, he felt so overwhelmed that he seriously considered resigning his leadership position. Late in the night, he went to his kitchen to pray for guidance and heard an inner voice saying, "Martin Luther, stand up for righteousness. Stand up for justice. Stand up for truth. And lo, I will be with you even unto the end of the world."

Strengthened by this transforming experience, King persevered, leading the boycott to a successful conclusion, which thrust him into national prominence. During the rest of his brief life, his activities were well reported. In 1957, he established the Southern Christian Leadership Conference, and in 1959, he visited India to learn more about Gandhi and his effective use of nonviolent strategies. The year 1963 was extremely consequential. Martin wrote the challenging "Letter from a Birmingham Jail," which castigated sincere white moderates for being "more devoted to order than to justice." He helped organize the March on Washington for Jobs and Freedom and delivered to some 250,000 demonstrators his "I Have a Dream" speech, which has continued to inspire efforts to work for social and economic equality in the United States. He opposed the Vietnam War in a speech at the Riverside Church in New York, which included this indictment: "A nation that continues to spend more money on military defense than on programs of social uplift is approaching spiritual death." This courageous moral stand, reinforced in later speeches, eventually cost him the support of his most powerful ally, President Lyndon Johnson.

Selma

In 1965, King led the bloody fifty-mile march from Selma to Montgomery, Alabama, which led to the passage of the federal Voting Rights Act that same year. In 1967, he helped plan the Poor People's March on Washington to persuade Congress to pass an economic bill of rights for poor Americans. Finally, in 1968, he came to the support of striking sanitation workers in Memphis, where he delivered his "I've Been to the Mountaintop" address and was assassinated the next day, April 4, 1968, by James Earl Ray. The death of the "drum major for justice" at age thirty-nine generated outrage and mourning throughout the country and the world.

Working for Justice

Martin Luther King continues to provide citizens of the United States with a compelling vision and solid reasons for participating in the quest for justice based on the American Dream and liberation themes in the Bible. In his first major public speech in December 1955, at the beginning of the Montgomery Bus Boycott, he argued that if the struggle to abolish Jim Crow laws was wrong, then "the Constitution is wrong" and "Jesus of Nazareth was merely a utopian dreamer." Throughout his all-too-brief life as a public theologian, King constructed many of his addresses around this fundamental strategy of correlating American ideals and relevant scriptural themes. In this way, he developed a distinctive North American liberation theology, designed to gain the support of white Americans in the struggle for racial and economic justice for all.

Dr. King insisted that we should work for justice because we are social creatures, interdependent persons who are responsible for one another. As he put it, "We are responsible human beings, not blind automatons; persons not puppets," who are "caught in an inescapable network of mutuality, tied in a single garment of destiny." We know the temptation to evade our responsibilities, but our true calling is to be faithful to "the drive for freedom," which moves us with "cosmic urgency" to create a more just and equitable world where all God's people enjoy economic opportunity and a share of political power.

A God of Justice and Mercy

King reminds us that the God who freed the Israelites from the cruel fate of slavery in Egypt and gave them social, economic, and political freedom calls us to participate in the crucial project of liberating both the oppressed and the oppressors from the enslavement of unjust dominating relationships. He imagines God not as a cosmic tyrant or an almighty monarch who deprives us of freedom but as the ultimately mysterious "benign Power," who has two outstretched arms, one "strong enough to surround us with justice" and the other "gentle enough to embrace us with grace." We enjoy "cosmic companionship" with this God who encourages us to temper the struggle for justice with tenderness and mercy.

The Sin of Dives

The inspiring sermons of the eloquent Baptist preacher encourage us to hear Christ's command to love our neighbor as a call to overcome the oppression of social sin and to create just institutions, systems, and structures that enable human beings to flourish. He encourages us to reflect on Christ as the Mediator, who makes it possible to relate to God in a personal way, and as the Exemplar of Humanity, who is "what every person must strive to be." In a sermon on the Gospel story of the rich man and Lazarus the poor man, King notes that the sin of Dives was not one of overt cruelty but of consistent omission: failing to notice Lazarus; lacking empathy for his situation; and, especially, accepting the fundamental inequality as normal and proper. He often applied this Gospel teaching to our current situation, pointing out that good people who fail to protest injustice are guilty of cooperating with it by their "appalling silence."

Role of the Church

According to Dr. King, the church, which is both a social institution and a religious community, has a moral responsibility "to save the soul of America" and to help establish the beloved community of justice and love. The church is called to expose the roots of prejudice based on fear and to overcome the false consciousness that supports unjust social institutions and structures. It should have an active program that helps to heal the brokenhearted and to liberate the oppressed. The church, which keeps alive the challenging memory of Jesus, should advocate nonviolent approaches in the struggle against powerful oppressive forces, meeting "physical force with soul force." As King makes clear, church membership should not shield us from the messy struggle for justice but should energize and motivate us to do our part to establish the beloved community where all can flourish.

Application

For the heroic icon of nonviolence, the Christian moral command to love our neighbor includes both personal conversion and social transformation. We are called to love our enemies, to do good to those who persecute us, and to go the extra mile in the pursuit of justice. Following the teaching of Jesus, we should put away the sword of violent confrontation and employ nonviolent civil disobedience to identify and transform sinful structures and patterns of discrimination. In the struggle for justice, the goal is not to defeat the oppressors but to win their understanding and cooperation in establishing a more equitable social order. King refined his Christian commitment to nonviolence through dialogue with Henry David Thoreau, Reinhold Niebuhr, and Mohandas Gandhi. He argues forcefully that Christ's law of love leaves no room for apathy, escapism, and passivity in the face of systematic injustice but calls for active engagement in the great project of creating a more equitable social order. Despite shattered dreams and personal disappointments, we must persevere in the pursuit of justice, hopeful that God remains with us, as promised, and that "the arc of the moral universe is long, but it bends toward justice."

As we have seen, the courageous life of Dr. Martin Luther King and his inspiring sermons and speeches provide a compelling vision of a mature Christian spirituality committed to the pursuit of justice. This vision is grounded on solid theology: we are social beings with communal responsibilities; God calls us to care for those who are marginalized; Christ commands us to love our enemies; the church has the task of creating the beloved community; Christian morality includes combating social sin; and God's promise of the final victory of justice will prevail over all the oppressive forces.

An Unsung Saint

I raise up as another advocate for justice my good friend Bernard J. Boff, who died in 2013 after more than fifty years of dedicated service as a priest of the Diocese of Toledo, Ohio. I first met Bernie in 1956 as a classmate at Mount St. Mary's Seminary in Cincinnati, where we formed lifelong bonds as young men coping, each in his own way, with the rigorous restrictions of seminary life and as teammates playing sports. After his ordination in 1961, Bernie became an associate pastor in a suburban parish where he took the initiative, without the permission of his pastor, to organize a group of parishioners to participate in the Christian Family Movement (CFM), designed to foster a lay spirituality dedicated to the works of charity and justice. Typically, a group of five couples met monthly in their homes to discuss the implications of belonging to the Mystical Body of Christ and to decide on a specific concrete action to help the needy and promote social justice. Following the traditional Observe–Judge–Act methodology, the participants worked on a chosen project during the month and reported on their progress at the next meeting. The task of the priest chaplain was to listen intently to the discussion and to conclude the meeting with an encouraging word and an appropriate prayer. My friend benefited greatly from this CFM experience, finding inspiration in the dedication of his parishioners and learning more about the challenges of creating a more just society.

An Urban Plunge

In the early 1960s, Bernie did an organized "urban plunge" in the inner city of Chicago, where he visited social service agencies, lived on a few dollars a day, and encountered the community-organizing tactics of Saul Alinsky. Drawing on this experience, Bernie established the Bible Center to serve the people living in the inner city of Toledo, Ohio. Volunteer teachers tutored area youngsters using the Montessori Method. During the summer, collegians came from around the region to canvas the neighborhood and interact with the poor. Bernie invited guest priests to preside at the daily celebration of the Eucharist, which exposed them to a new world and provided spiritual nourishment for the participants.

Selma

In 1965, when Martin Luther King's first effort to march from Selma to Montgomery was thwarted by a vicious attack by police on "Bloody Sunday," Dr. King asked clergy and other supporters to come to Selma to participate in another march. On March 15, Bernie Boff, along with some other Toledo priests, answered that call and went to Selma, where they participated in the first part of the successful march to Montgomery, which led to the passage of the Voting Rights Act of 1965. Later, Bernie recalled his trepidation as Dr. King announced the beginning of the march and his relief when the first phase proved to be peaceful.

Resurrection City

Always attuned to the cause of justice for the poor, Bernie watched closely the 1968 Poor People's Campaign, planned by Dr. King and carried out after his assassination, which demanded economic justice for poor Americans. Participants in the march to Washington set up a tent city on the Washington Mall, known as Resurrection City, which provided shelter for the initial three thousand residents, mostly poor people from around the country. Sensing some of the practical needs of the residents, Fr. Boff, with the help of three young black men, loaded up his station wagon with food and drove to Washington, where they distributed the food and lived in the tent city for a few days. The Poor People's Campaign did not succeed in getting economic rights legislation passed, and Resurrection City had many internal problems; but Bernie's limited participation served as a symbolic action, expressing his solidarity with poor people everywhere and his commitment to helping the needy in Toledo.

Mission in Zimbabwe

From 1987 to 2001, Bernie served as director of the Office of Global Concerns, which gave him a platform for promoting the diocesan Mission of Accompaniment, which involved a working relationship between the Toledo Diocese and the Diocese of Hwange, Zimbabwe. Bernie visited our mission team there six times and developed a great love and respect for the native BaTonga people. Along with a courageous missionary, Ruth Ann Leidorf, Bernie wrote a book, *Surprises of the Spirit*, explaining the ideal of "reverse mission," which recognizes that missionaries both teach and learn and that cultural exchanges are mutually enriching. Reflecting on his experience with the BaTonga people, he highlighted their great generosity, even when suffering the cross of deprivation.

When Bernie died on August 8, 2013, after a decade of patiently accepting the diminishments of Parkinson's disease, I was honored to preach at his funeral Mass. In my homily, which emphasized our common vocation to follow Christ by taking up our cross daily, I raised up my friend as a man with a "cruciform heart," who bore his own crosses gracefully and had an instinctive empathy for those suffering from the cross of injustice. Bernard J. Boff continues to be for me and others who knew him an enduring reminder that Christian holiness must include the pursuit of justice.

6

Time for Prayer

In the exhortation, Pope Francis states that "holiness consists in a habitual openness to the transcendent, expressed in prayer and adoration." The saints "find an exclusive concern with this world to be narrow and stifling, and, amid their own concerns and commitments, they long for God, losing themselves in praise and contemplation of the Lord." The pope adds, "I do not believe in holiness without prayer, even though that prayer need not be lengthy or invoke intense emotions" (no. 147). Francis encourages us to develop the habit of "prayerful silence," not as an escape from the world but as a time of "solitary converse" with the Lord, when we recall our many blessings, offer petitions for others, and discern our own distinctive path to holiness (nos. 149–54). Prayerful engagement with Scripture and participation in the Eucharist strengthen and guide our efforts to sanctify our everyday lives (nos. 156–57).

However, Francis warns us: "It is not healthy to love silence while fleeing interactions with others, to want peace and quiet while avoiding activity, to seek prayer while disdaining service." We are called to a more integrated spirituality, "to be contemplatives even in the midst of action and to grow in holiness by responsibly and generously carrying out our proper mission" (no. 26). Maintaining this posture is especially difficult in today's world, with its heavy demands, superficial pleasures, and "endless array of consumer goods." We may "fail to realize the need to stop this rat race and to recover the personal space needed to carry on a heartfelt dialogue with God" (no. 29). To counter this temptation, "we need a spirit of holiness capable of filling both our solitude and our service, our personal life and our evangelizing efforts, so that every moment can be an expression of self-sacrificing love in the Lord's eyes. In this way, every minute of our lives can be a step along the path to growth in holiness" (no. 31). Following the advice of Pope Francis, we can grow spiritually by maintaining "contemplation in action," by balancing prayer and everyday activities, by creating a synergistic interaction between interior reflection and external activity, and by integrating love of God and love of neighbor.

A CELEBRATED SAINT

To better appreciate contemplation in action, let us explore the life and thought of the former secretary-general of the United Nations, Dag Hammarskjöld (1905–1961). Dag was born into a prestigious family, the youngest son of the man who served as prime minister of Sweden from 1914 to 1917. He grew up in Uppsala. In 1930, he earned a law degree from Uppsala University and, in 1936, a doctorate in economics from Stockholm University. His career as a public servant and government official included chairing the Swedish delegation to the U.N. General Assembly in New York in 1952. A year later, he was elected as secretary-general of the United Nations. He threw himself into his new position, meeting world leaders and establishing personal relationships with his staff and leaders in the various U.N. departments. He got very involved in creating a meditation room, a Room of Silence, on the first floor in the U.N. headquarters in New York, where people of all faiths could spend time in silent prayer. He traveled extensively, including a visit to China to negotiate the release of eleven U.S. pilots captured during the Korean War. Much of his energy was spent trying to improve relations between Israel and its Arab neighbors.

The Suez Canal

Dag played a major role in achieving a peaceful resolution of the Suez Canal crisis of 1956 and 1957, when Egyptian president Nasser nationalized the Suez Canal, prompting English, French, and Israeli troops to invade the Canal Zone. In a risky and innovative move, Hammarskjöld got the General Assembly to establish and employ, for the first time, a U.N. Emergency Force to maintain a ceasefire agreement in the Canal Zone.

From July 1960, when the Congo achieved independence from Belgium, Hammarskjöld was totally immersed in halting the Congolese civil war and in preventing it from escalating into an armed confrontation between the Soviet Union and Western allies. Unfortunately, he died unexpectedly when his plane mysteriously crashed on September 18, 1961, while on his way to negotiate a cease-fire in that troubled country.

The Statesman

Dag Hammarskjöld was indeed a man of action. As the second secretary-general of the United Nations, he worked long hours, often with little sleep, engaging in shuttle diplomacy, managing his large U.N. staff, meeting with world leaders, attending conferences, giving speeches, entertaining diplomats, corresponding with a large group of friends and colleagues, dealing with the press, and making formal reports to the Security Council and the General Assembly. President Eisenhower once praised him as a man with remarkable "physical stamina," who works all day long "intelligently and devotedly" with only a few hours' sleep. In his personal interactions with others, he had an amazing ability to be totally present, to read body language, and to discern emotional nuance. In times of crisis, he maintained a calm demeanor, a clear sense of purpose, and an openness to creative solutions. President John Kennedy spoke

for many when he called Hammarskjöld the "greatest
statesman of our century."

Spiritual Life

While Hammarskjöld's public service was widely reported
and appreciated by many, his deep spiritual life was largely
unrecognized. He did give significant clues in some of his
public statements, especially a November 1953 presentation on Edward R. Murrow's radio program, *This I Believe*.
In his prepared statement, he affirmed his honest adult
appropriation of the beliefs he received as a youth: the virtue of selfless, courageous public service from his father;
and from his mother's side, the radical gospel teaching to
treat others as equal children of God. He raised up Albert
Schweitzer (1875–1965), the theologian and missionary
physician to equatorial Africa, as a prime example of a
gospel-based life of service to those in need.

The Mystics

For directions on how to combine a deep inner life and a
life of active service, Hammarskjöld turned to the great
medieval mystics, who insisted that self-surrender is the
key to self-realization and to meeting the demands and
duties of life, whatever the personal cost. He ended his
statement of belief by insisting that what the mystics discovered about "the laws of inner life and of action" remain
relevant for the modern world.

Markings

After Hammarskjöld's tragic death in 1961, his diary, which was later published under the title *Markings*, was discovered in his house in New York. With it was a letter to a friend that gave permission to publish it and described it "as a sort of white book concerning my negotiations with myself and with God." In the journal, he called his entries "signposts," which he hoped would be of interest, but only if what he wrote "has an honesty without trace of vanity or self-regard."

When the English version of *Markings*, with a somewhat critical foreword by the poet W. H. Auden, first appeared in 1964, it immediately became a bestseller and generated thoughtful reviews in many publications, including the *New York Times*, lauding Hammarskjöld as a "revered statesman" and a man of "quite extraordinary inner life." In his foreword, Auden captured the abiding significance of *Markings* as a unique account of the effort of a professional person "to unite in one life the *via activa* and the *via contemplativa*," the spiritual life of prayerful reflection and the active life of public service.

Loneliness

Throughout *Markings*, Hammarskjöld speaks openly and honestly about his great cross in life, an abiding sense of loneliness, a deep anguish that he considered almost inevitable given his personality and his vocational choice not to get married. So intense was the sense of aloneness that he periodically considered suicide. At times, he said, "it seems so much more difficult to live than to die." In his darkest moments, he prayed that his loneliness would spur him to find something to live for and a cause great enough to die for. Ultimately, it was his faith in God that enabled him to overcome his suicidal thoughts and to transform his loneliness into a life of service.

He was relentless in his effort to face the dark side of his inner life: pride, vanity, self-importance, the desire for fame, the need to impress others, envy, work as an escape, and all inner self-deception. He reminded himself to "gaze steadfastly" at these destructive tendencies until he plumbed their depths. He wanted to understand "Original Sin," the "dark counter-center of evil in our nature" that distorts our thinking and action. He reminded himself not to brood over his "pettiness with masochistic self-disgust," but to be mindful of it as a "threat to my integrity of action."

Biblical Teaching

In dealing with his personal demons, Hammarskjöld drew on the biblical tradition familiar to him from his Swedish Lutheran background. *Markings*, for example, has many short quotes from the Book of Psalms that offer guidance and comfort: "Give not yourselves unto vanity" (62:10); and "I will lay me down in peace, and take my rest: for it is thou, Lord, only that makes me dwell in safety" (4:8).

His journal has an extended Gospel-based reflection on Christ as an "adamant young man," who washed the feet of his disciples at the Last Supper and who faced death "without self-pity or demand for sympathy, fulfilling the destiny" he had chosen. Several times, he reflected on Christ's agony in Gethsemane, when his friends fell asleep and God was silent. Jesus could relate to outcasts because his humanity was "rich and deep enough" to make contact with their common humanity. Although Dag emphasized Christ's humanity, he was also able to address him as "Thou," the Son of God, who remains with the human family and walks with us on our journey.

Prayers

Markings is full of prayers composed or adapted by Hammarskjöld. Reflecting on the Lord's Prayer, he wrote "Hallowed be Thy name, not mine, Thy Kingdom come, not mine, Thy will be done, not mine." Some of his prayers address God in explicit trinitarian terms: "Before Thee Father, in righteousness and humility, With Thee, Brother, in faith and courage, In Thee, Spirit, in stillness." He had a clear sense of his total dependency on the God who wants us to be freely responsible for our lives. The great statesman who said, "Not I, but God in me!" also wrote, "God desires our independence—which we attain when, ceasing to strive for it ourselves, we fall back into God." As these examples indicate, much of Hammarskjöld's spirituality reflects a solid biblical grounding in his Lutheran heritage. There was, however, another side to his inner life that, as he himself indicated in his personal creed, drew inspiration from the medieval mystics.

Mystical Experience

Scholars debate whether Hammarskjöld was himself a mystic, but this entry in his journal clearly reflects the typical mystical sense of undifferentiated unity. "In a dream I walked with God through the deep places of creation, past walls that receded and gates that opened, through hall after hall of silence, darkness and refreshment—the dwelling place of souls acquainted with light and warmth—until around me, was an infinity into which all flowed together and lived anew."

Meister Eckhart

Among the Catholic mystics, Dag's favorite author was Meister Eckhart (1260–1328), the German theologian, who taught at the University of Paris, served as a Dominican provincial, preached widely, and wrote extensively. In his preaching, he emphasized detachment and self-emptying as well as the human capacity to receive God's "overabundant love." Eckhart stands as a prime example of a contemplative in action, a busy Christian leader and scholar fueled by an extremely rich inner life.

Hammarskjöld directly quoted Eckhart at least nine times in *Markings*, with many other indirect allusions to his thought. In an entry on Christmas Eve, 1956, he quotes from Eckhart: "If, without any side glances, we have only God in view . . . Such a man does not seek rest, for he is not troubled by any unrest . . . He must acquire an inner solitude, no matter where or with whom he may be: he must learn to pierce the veil of things and comprehend God *within them*." The next day, on Christmas, he again quoted the Dominican theologian, who recommended detachment from all outward things: "You must have an exalted mind and a *burning* heart in which, nevertheless, reign silence and stillness."

Clearly, he resonated with major themes of Eckhart and the mystical tradition. The true God is incomprehensible beyond all reasoning and imagining. The one God is the inexhaustible source of our inner energy and the goal of our deepest longings. Self-forgetfulness is the key to the self-fulfillment God wills for us. We are totally dependent on God in serving as instruments of the divine will. There is an essential unity of all created reality held together by God's loving embrace. Solitude and silence are crucial to spiritual growth and effective efforts to spread God's kingdom. As did Eckhart, Hammarskjöld developed a spirituality that fruitfully combined a deep interior life with a demanding life of action.

Yes to God

The secretary-general, however, did have his own unique way of appropriating and living the mystical tradition. In a journal entry on Whitsunday, 1961, he made the revealing confession:

> I don't know Who—or what—put the question, I
> don't know when it was put. I don't even remember
> answering. But at some moment I did answer *Yes*
> to Someone—or Something—and from that hour
> I was certain that existence is meaningful and that,
> therefore, my life, in self-surrender, had a goal.

Although the historical dynamics of his vocational response remain obscure, the significant point is that he found meaning in his life of self-surrender by making an affirmative response to a transcendent reality. In other words, suggested by other entries, his *yes* to God's call enabled him to carry his personal crosses and to live a productive life of generous public service. In another significant entry, he expressed his fundamental acceptance of his evolving life: "For all that has been—Thanks! To all that shall be—Yes!"

Inner Life

The secretary-general clearly understood the spiritual significance of his extremely demanding leadership position: "In our era, the road to holiness necessarily passes through the world of action." At the same time, he knew intuitively that cultivating his spiritual life was crucial to sanctifying his public life. Experience taught him the great challenge of maintaining a vital inner life, expressed in his statement: "The longest journey is inward." The rewards are great, however, for finding "the point of rest at the center of our being" where "a tree becomes a mystery, a cloud a revelation, each man a cosmos of whose riches we can only catch a glimpse." This same center point enabled him to stay calm in the midst of international crises, to function effectively on little sleep, and to make prudent decisions on behalf of justice and peace.

Biography

In his masterful 2016 biography, *Hammarskjöld: A Life*, scholar Roger Lipsey explores the synergistic relationship between Hammarskjöld's inner life and his dedicated public service. He detects a general methodology that Dag developed through his adult life, "a practice of self-observation," or "conscious self-scrutiny," that enabled him to achieve a deeper self-knowledge and to mobilize his talents to make a difference in the world. Dag himself put it this way: "The more faithfully you listen to the voice inside you, the better you will hear what is sounding outside." Such intense listening requires silence or "stillness," a term borrowed from Eckhart, which is absolutely necessary for an authentic life of service to others. When an interviewer inquired about the main qualities of an international leader, Hammarskjöld mentioned a "heightened awareness combined with an inner quiet," along with a humility that respects the perspectives of others.

Lipsey notes that in the early 1950s, Hammarskjöld

began using the term "the unheard of" to point to the transcendent dimension present in everyday life. It is through a "life of sacrifice" and personal "surrender" that one can break down the illusory walls that divide us from the unheard of transcendent and perform public service that fosters peace in the world.

Hammarskjöld wrote of both his dedication to public life and his awareness of the dynamics of his inner life. "We all have within us a center of stillness surrounded by silence." Attention to this center point is crucial because God's "orders are given in secret." He relied on "intuitive rediscovery," an awareness of the divine presence that guided his decisions on international relations as well as his ongoing process of self-exploration. As a believing Christian, he was grateful for God's initiative, "for being allowed to listen, to observe, to understand." It was the same faith perspective that energized and guided his challenging vocation as secretary-general of the United Nations.

Contribution

Challenging Auden's charge that Hammarskjöld lacked "originality of insight," Roger Lipsey noted his distinctive appropriation of medieval mysticism. "He had integrated depth of inner life with mastery of political processes. He had done so as a man of the modern West, a Christian and humanist open to the world's political wisdom and spirituality. This was his astonishing achievement and contribution."[1] In a 1953 radio address, with a message for all of us seeking to integrate our inner and outer lives, the secretary-general insisted:

> Our work for peace must begin within the private world of each one of us. To build for man a world without fear, we must be without fear. To build a world of justice, we must be just. And how can we fight for liberty if we are not free in our own minds? How can we ask others to sacrifice if we are not ready to do so? Some might consider this to be just another expression of noble principles, too far from the harsh realities of political life . . . I disagree. (UN Press Release SG/360, December 22, 1953)

In a journal entry just months before his death, Dag Hammarskjöld addressed a prayer to "Thou Whom I do not comprehend but Who hast dedicated me to my fate." This prayer of a great statesman and a true contemplative in action invites us to share in his quest for an integrated spirituality. "Give us a pure heart that we may see Thee, a humble heart that we may hear Thee, a heart of love that we may serve Thee, a heart of faith that we may live Thee."

AN UNSUNG SAINT

In trying to integrate prayer and action in our busy lives, I find another inspiring example in my longtime friend

---

1. Roger Lipsey, *Hammarskjöld: A Life* (Ann Arbor, MI: University of Michigan Press, 2013), 608.

Mary, who has effectively managed her busy and extremely challenging life by maintaining a deep, prayerful spirituality. The youngest of five children, Mary was born into a devout German Catholic family in Ottawa, Ohio. When she was three, her father was killed in a tragic automobile accident, leaving her with just family stories of a good man she never got to know. Her mother did all she could to support Mary and her siblings, doing odd jobs, such as cleaning houses and taking in laundry. A good student, Mary attended a local Catholic school for twelve years. After graduating from high school, she could not afford to go to college, so she took a job in a nearby town, making good money. Shortly after, she fell in love with a fine man, who was divorced following a very brief marriage and loved her deeply. However, she made a very difficult decision to break off the relationship because, at the time, she saw no way to marry him in the church and knew that she could not be happy alienated from her Catholic faith.

Marriage and Family

Partly to get distance from this relationship and partly to satisfy her innate adventuresome spirit, Mary moved to California, where she found a great job with a large insurance company that brought her a good deal of personal satisfaction.

After a little over a year, she returned to Ohio for her brother's graduation from college and, for various reasons, never returned to California. Back home, she joined the

Air Force, hoping that it would enable her to travel and eventually provide the opportunity for a college education under the GI Bill. She did her basic training in San Antonio and was assigned to an airbase in Denver, where she fell in love with Kim, a combat veteran, who was raised Mormon but converted to Catholicism. About a year later, they were married in the Catholic Church in Ottawa. Ten months to the day after their wedding, Mary gave birth to twin boys and just over a year later brought another set of twin boys into the world, leaving her with four young children before her second wedding anniversary. She found strength for this demanding responsibility by maintaining her practice of participating in Sunday liturgy and her regular daily prayer routine.

At some point, Mary and her family moved to Bowling Green, Ohio, where Kim, with her full support and encouragement, attended classes at the local university, completed a degree, and got a job teaching at a nearby high school, which he loved. During those years, they had three more children and formed an effective loving partnership in raising them in the Catholic faith and managing household affairs. They were very involved in their parish, with both teaching CCD classes and Kim serving as a lector, as well as sending their kids to the parish grade school.

Tragedy

It was about thirteen years into their happy marriage that Kim was killed in a tragic car accident. Strengthened by her Catholic faith, Mary buried her beloved husband and took on the challenge of raising seven young children by herself. Coping with her husband's death was immensely challenging. She endured sleepless nights, uncontrollable emotions, and frightening nightmares. At times she struggled just to make it through the day and remain sane. Attending Mass brought a measure of comfort, but also unleashed a flood of tears, usually after receiving communion. Through it all, she found comfort in the words Paul wrote to the Romans: "How unsearchable are his judgments and how inscrutable his ways! 'For who has known the mind of the Lord? Or who has been his counselor?'" (Rom 11:33–34).

Education and Employment

With little time to grieve properly, she made a crucial decision to start taking classes at the university, partly to maintain her sanity and partly to prepare for a teaching career to support herself and her children. Utilizing her considerable organizational skills, she managed to care for her kids (the older ones became quite self-sufficient and helped with the younger ones), and in about five years, she earned a degree and got a job teaching fourth grade in a local public school.

Theological Development

Soon after Kim's death, Mary decided that she had not only to provide for herself financially but also try to enrich her spiritual life. To this end, she participated in a course I was teaching on the German Jesuit theologian Karl Rahner. My initial encounter with Mary in the class was very positive, as I knew something of her challenging situation and recognized the seriousness of her pursuit of a spirituality that would enable her to function on a daily basis. She was very taken with Rahner's emphasis on the incomprehensibility of God, who is beyond all our thoughts and images, and with his insistence that accepting this limitation actually brings us closer to God. Rahner's theology of death also proved helpful to her, especially his notion that our deceased loved ones not only live with God but also continue to be with us and for us, which she applied to her husband, Kim. She resonated with Rahner's insight that calm acceptance is the key to spiritual growth and maturity, acceptance of blessings and disappointments, achievements and failures, joys and sorrows.

After Mary taught grade school for a number of years, she returned to do graduate studies at Bowling Green State University, earning a master's degree in education with a specialty in reading, which enabled her to get a job in a public school helping youngsters develop their reading skills.

A Second Marriage

After twelve years of living as a widow, Mary found another loving partner, Marv, a practicing Presbyterian,

a corporate executive, and a former catcher in the Yan-
kees farm system. He loved her, supported her, attended
Mass with her, prayed at night with her, and befriended
her children, enjoying vacations and fun times together.
About thirty-five years into her happy second marriage,
Mary had to deal with another devastating tragedy. Her
second oldest son, one of the twins, was diagnosed with
lung cancer and died shortly after. This was the most
heart-wrenching cross she ever had to bear, and only her
Catholic faith enabled her to survive and carry on. Just
months later, her husband Marv died a peaceful death.
She not only grieved his passing but also, at the same
time, grieved more thoroughly than ever before the loss
of her first husband, Kim. Once again, it was her faith
that enabled her to manage this mysterious combination
of two deeply emotional marital losses.

Her Journal

It was about six years into her first marriage that Mary
started keeping a journal, which gives glimpses of the
spirituality that sustained her in good times and bad.
Through her whole life, participating in the Eucharist
has been the solid constant in her spirituality. Even in the
worst of times, she never missed Sunday Mass. Somehow,
she got seven kids to Mass every Sunday, even the Sunday after Kim died. During the most demanding times,
the Sunday Eucharist provided nourishment for her soul,

giving her motivation and energy for the week ahead. Receiving communion is the high point of the liturgy for her. Her devotion to Christ present in the Eucharist now issues in her weekly practice of spending an hour before the Blessed Sacrament in silent prayer of praise, gratitude, and petition.

Prayer

During her adulthood, Mary has engaged in what we can call situational prayer, short prayers addressed to God in the midst of busy days. When things went well with her kids, she said, "Thank you, Lord." When faced with dark moments of tragedy, anxiety, and worry, she asked, "Lord, please give me strength." When struggling to deal with her teenage boys, she sought guidance: "Holy Spirit, give me the right words." When she was teaching, she prayed, "Lord, fill me with so much love for you that it will spill over to everyone I see today."

Throughout her life, her prayer has focused on doing God's will. In her journal, she wrote, "Please, Lord, help me to pray. Help me to learn to know you better and to know your will, or to do your will even though I don't understand it. Please, Lord, help me." We see here her sense of the incomprehensibility of God, which she found in Rahner's theology. Mary was always interested in improving her prayer life. In her journal, she recalls reading Fr. Edward Farrell's book *Prayer Is a Hunger*, which emphasized communing with God daily and personally writing about it, which she did in her journal. In an early entry, she responded to a question raised in the Rahner class about our primary positive intuition in life: "Somehow I believe in a Real Power governing (not withstanding my own free will) my life. It is more than a belief; it is a sure knowledge arrived at from having seen it manifested so many times in my life."

Her Catholic Faith

Mary's journal reveals how deeply she thought about her Catholic faith. She saw the sacrament of Penance not so much as confessing a list of sins but as assessing who we are and how God sees us "stripped of various masks." At times, she thought how great it would be to join a contemplative order and "just read and pray and write," but then she realized that human relationships, messy as they are, bring forth the best in us.

She developed a thirst for Scripture, eager to read "every bit of the epistles and every word Jesus said in the Gospels." Reading the Acts of the Apostles reminded her that she is part of a long tradition going back to the early church. For her, Christ was fully human, like us in all things but sin, so that we can identify with him and try to imitate his good example. In one of her later entries, she wrote, "I feel good about being a Catholic," recalling how her faith strengthened her in difficult times. In retrospect, she thinks the theology of Karl Rahner gave her a solid base for continuing her lifelong quest to be a faithful disciple of Christ.

Religious Experience

Later in her life, Mary recalled a number of what she called "Eureka moments"—times when God was especially present to her. Holding one of her newborn sons for the first time, she felt an awesome sense of "having a share in creation." One winter day, she had a "breathtaking spiritual experience," when "the trees were covered with hoarfrost and the bright sunshine turned them into jeweled giants." Decades after the event, she still recalled a vivid memory of the first time she saw the Pacific Ocean, "magnificent in all its azure splendor," with foamy whitecaps lapping the shore. While in Hawaii, she silently contemplated "the vast wonder" of Waimea Canyon, hoping none of her companions would break the silence. Fulfilling a lifelong dream, Mary made a pilgrimage to the Holy Land "to walk the very paths that Our Lord had trod," which proved to be a "rewarding experience" but not quite up to what she had anticipated and not striking enough to make the Eureka list. Back home, however, during her weekly hour of prayer before the Blessed Sacrament, she had a true Eureka moment, realizing that she did not have to travel across the ocean to find the Savior because he is right here, as he always was in all the challenges and joys of her life.

Application

My friend Mary serves as an especially poignant example of the power of Catholic spirituality to meet the challenges of everyday life in our busy modern world. She developed what can be called a "structured-situational" spirituality, which has enabled her to cope with tragedy and the challenges of her demanding life. Regular attendance at Sunday Mass has been her touchstone, her structured routine, that has nourished her soul and solidified her faith perspective on life. Her intuitive habit of saying short prayers throughout the day has provided meaning and energy for meeting the demands of everyday life. Her prayer life enabled her to survive tragedy, maintain hope, and meet the individual needs of her family. Mary's story encourages us to find our own form of a spirituality, which includes a repeatable spiritual exercise (liturgy, Scripture reading, meditation, examination of conscience) and encourages greater attention to God's activity in our daily lives, leading to brief prayers of praise, gratitude, and petition.

7

Caring for the Needy

In *Gaudete et Exultate*, Pope Francis includes a section entitled "The Great Criterion," which expands the beatitude "Blessed are the merciful" (Matt 25:31–46), where Jesus identifies himself with persons who are hungry, thirsty, strangers, naked, sick, and imprisoned (nos. 95–105). This passage in Matthew, which "offers us one clear criterion on which we will be judged," reveals "the very heart of Christ, his deepest feelings and choices, which every saint seeks to imitate." Francis insists that "holiness cannot be understood or lived apart from these demands, for mercy is the beating heart of the Gospel." Our worship is pleasing to God when it "nourishes a daily commitment to love" and "concern for our brothers and sisters." Treating those in need with mercy is "the very foundation of the Church's life," the "most radiant manifestation of God's truth" and "the key to heaven."

A Celebrated Saint

In our own times, we are blessed with a familiar, inspiring example of a Matthew 25 spirituality in St. Teresa of Calcutta—Mother Teresa as she is known to many around the world. Born on August 27, 1910, she was the third child of Catholic Albanian parents living as a minority in Skopje, Macedonia (then part of the Ottoman Empire), where she attended public schools and took religion classes in her local parish. "From childhood the Heart of Jesus has been my first love," she recalled years later in a letter to one of her spiritual confidants and added in a subsequent letter, "From the age of 5½, when I first received Him, the love for souls has been within." By the age of twelve, she knew she wanted to be a missionary to the poor. When she was eighteen, she left a very happy home life to join the Sisters of Our Lady of Loreto. Forty years later, she wrote, "I've never doubted even for a second that I've done the right thing; it was the will of God. It was His choice."

The "Saint of Calcutta" made her final vows as a Sister of Loreto on May 24, 1937. In a letter to a priest in her hometown, she expressed some of her deeper feelings on the occasion: "How happy I was that I could, of my own free will, ignite my own sacrifice." She now saw herself as "the spouse of Jesus" and declared, "I would give everything, even life itself, for Him." She carried out her spousal commitment by teaching at St. Mary's High School in Calcutta and later serving as principal. In April 1942, her desire for closer union with God drove her to make a secret private vow to God binding herself under pain of mortal sin "to give to God anything that He may ask, not to refuse Him anything." This secret vow, rooted in her total trust in God's unconditional love, gave her a great sense of inner joy and a cheerful spirit in serving others.

Serving the Poorest of the Poor

On September 10, 1946, Mother Teresa was traveling by train to a retreat site when Christ called her "to go out in the streets to serve the poorest of the poor." It was "a call within a call" to satiate the thirst of Jesus, a reference to his cry on the cross, "I thirst," which she interpreted as an infinite thirst for love and souls. During the next ten months, Mother Teresa had many intimate conversations with Jesus, who addressed her as "my own spouse," pleading with her: "Come, come carry Me into the holes of the poor. Come, be My Light." Jesus often punctuated the plea by asking, "Wilt thou refuse?" Not only did she hear the voice of the Lord, she also had vivid visions. In the most significant one, she is a little child standing with Mary facing Jesus on the cross. She sees a great crowd of children and poor people covered in darkness, and Jesus says, "Will you refuse to do this for Me, to take care of them, to bring them to Me?" She answers, "You know, Jesus, I am ready to go at a minute's notice."

The Missionaries of Charity

In August 1948, Mother Teresa finally received permission from Rome to leave the Loreto Sisters and respond to the call she was sure came from the Lord. Thus began her ministry to the poorest of the poor. Her story became familiar to the world: the demanding daily routine of prayer and selfless service to the homeless in Calcutta; the founding of the Missionaries of Charity, who eventually had houses in over a hundred countries; being awarded the Nobel Peace Prize; her death on September 5, 1997, at age eighty-seven; her state funeral provided by the Indian government and televised to millions around the world; and her canonization as a saint by Pope Francis on September 4, 2016. Mother Teresa relied on the Spirit of the risen Christ to guide and empower her. The gospel summons to take up the cross and follow Jesus shaped her consciousness and inflamed her heart. She manifested in her own life the essential Christian paradox: if we die with Christ, we will also rise with him to a new and richer life.

Matthew 25

She accepted a simple but profound theology that empha-sizes the essential connection between the Eucharist and a life of service. With the eyes of faith, she was able to see Jesus in both the bread consecrated at Mass and the faces of the poor. Chapter 25 of Matthew's Gospel, where Jesus identifies himself with those who are hungry, thirsty, imprisoned, and homeless, totally captured her imagina-tion. It grounded her faith and sustained her dedication to service. It enabled her to see Jesus in "the distressing disguise of the poorest of the poor," as the rule of her order states. Serving Christ in others became for Mother Teresa a way of life. It was her key to understanding the human condition and coping with human suffering. She believed that the sufferings of the innocent are joined with the sufferings of Jesus for the betterment of the entire human family.

Solidly grounded in this faith conviction, Mother Teresa followed the Master in exercising genuine compassion toward individuals in need. Her service to others manifests no hint of a detached philanthropy that considers the poor as objects of charity. Nor did she fall into a sentimental pity that treats outcasts merely as unfortunate victims. With a sober and practical realism, this strong-willed woman sought out those most in need and treated them as individual persons, possessing an inherent dignity and worth. She had a deep respect for the spiritual sensibilities of the people she served, mostly Hindus and Muslims. Her goal was to comfort them, not to convert them. She often reminded her sisters that they have much to learn from the poor and that they should serve them with joy, mindful that they receive more from the outcasts of society than they could ever give them.

Relating to Christ

Mother Teresa's ability to see Jesus in others was closely connected with her abiding awareness of the presence of Christ in her own soul. Her passion was to empty herself so that Jesus could grow in her mind and heart. She saw herself as an instrument of the Lord, who accomplished good things through her. Her daily Eucharist and regular private prayer nourished her spiritual life and sharpened her awareness of the presence of Jesus in herself and others.

This close personal relationship with Christ served as the real foundation for her Matthew 25 spirituality. It enabled her to put aside her own interests and to concentrate on the needs of the people she met and served. Her faith allowed her to respond calmly to the critics who wanted her to concentrate more on transforming unjust institutions. Quite simply, she felt very confident that Christ called her to care for the poorest of the poor, one person at a time. At the same time, she hoped that others would respond to their distinctive calling to challenge oppressive structures.

Impact

Mother Teresa made such a positive impact on others because she radiated the peace of Christ in her own heart and because she saw Jesus in all the people she met. She appropriated an essential truth of the gospel and lived it wholeheartedly. Her total dedication to serving the poor inspired many generous people to join her in that mission. Her personal integrity and joyful spirit helped many more to appreciate anew the gospel mandate to practice charity in ordinary life. She enriched the human family, not by grandiose accomplishments but by her simple sanctity and her oft-repeated invitation "to do something beautiful for God."

Inner Emptiness

It was some years after the death of Mother Teresa, in 1997, when we first learned about the mostly hidden story of her interior spiritual life. The publication of *Mother Teresa: Come Be My Light*, which was edited with a commentary by Fr. Brian Kolodiejchuk, the advocate for her canonization, made pubic many private letters that the Saint of Calcutta wrote to various spiritual confidants. They reveal her protracted struggle with an agonizing interior darkness, what *Time* magazine called "a beloved icon's 50-year crisis of faith."

From the time she embarked on her "call within a call," Mother Teresa's inner life took a dramatic, wrenching turn. She no longer heard the voice of "her spouse" or experienced any more visions. The comforting warmth of her relationship to Jesus turned to ice. Over the course of five decades, she periodically tried to describe her interior darkness to various spiritual directors. She wrote of feeling alone, unwanted, forsaken. When she tried to raise her thoughts to heaven, "there is such convicting emptiness that those very thoughts return like sharp knives and hurt my very soul . . . I am told God loves me and yet the reality of darkness and coldness and emptiness is so great that nothing touches my soul."[1] People who encounter her joyful spirit think that intimacy with God absorbs her heart, but really "cheerfulness is the cloak by which I cover the emptiness and misery." She suffers from "pains without ceasing" and "untold agony" and is afraid to uncover the "many unanswered questions" that "live within me."

The darkness and emptiness are horrible but even worse is the pain of her intense "longing for God." The tremendous contradiction between her desire for God and God's absence is so sharp that she fears that it "will unbalance me." She worries about being hypocritical since she speaks to others about the "tender love of God" and yet "no light of inspiration enters my soul," leaving her with the "terrible pain of loss of God not wanting me."

Accepting the Darkness

In 1961, one of her more astute spiritual directors, Fr. Joseph Neuner, advised her that "the only response to this trial is the total surrender to God and the acceptance of the darkness in union with Jesus." She took his advice and reported that for the first time in eleven years she came "to love the darkness," and this brought her "a deep joy." Although the darkness continued to assail her the rest of her life (with one five-week respite after the death of Pope

---

1. Mother Teresa, *Mother Teresa: Come Be My Light*, ed. Brian Kolodiejchuk (New York: Image, 2013), 187.

Pius XII in 1958), she accepted it and was able to carry on her ministry to the poor with a cheerful spirit and a radiant smile on her face.

Analysis

How are we to understand Mother Teresa's portrayal of her inner spiritual life? All religious experiences are personally and culturally conditioned. Throughout Christian history, saints have described their encounters with the ultimately mysterious God in words, images, and categories familiar to them. Since Mother Teresa thought of her relationship to Jesus in spousal terms, it is not surprising that she heard Jesus address her as "my spouse." Her tremendous capacity for self-giving love disposed her to interpret God's love for her as an ever-greater call for self-sacrifice. Her own natural instinct to help one poor person at a time may explain why she heard no divine call to challenge the unjust structures and systems that imprison so many in poverty. Her passionate desire to love Jesus more than he has ever been loved sets the stage for his oft-repeated question to her: "Wilt thou refuse me?" Because she saw Christ in the Eucharist, she could see the poor as Christ in disguise.

When Mother Teresa writes with great anguish about Jesus still suffering today because poor persons and little children are not being saved, we can recognize her own theological outlook rather than assume this is a divinely revealed truth. Suggestions that God was testing her love with those horrible spiritual torments is likewise

theologically questionable. Perhaps her dark night was
rooted in her tremendous capacity for empathy. She had
a profound sympathy for the crucified Christ, who felt
abandoned by God. She often spoke of the great suffering of the poor who were left alone and unloved. We can
imagine her deep identification with Christ and the poor
predisposing her to participate spiritually in their sense
of abandonment. She herself wrote, "The physical situation of my poor left in the streets unwanted, unloved,
unclaimed are the true picture of my own spiritual life."
Whatever the mysterious dynamic of her interior suffering, the truly remarkable fact, both instructive and
inspiring, is that Mother Teresa carried on her mission
to the poorest of the poor for half a century without
spiritual consolation but always with a hearty yes to
God and a big smile for all.

Criticisms

Saint Teresa had her critics. For example, feminist Ger-
maine Greer accused her of being a vain headline-grab-
bing jet-setter, who did more harm than good by creating
the impression that Hindu India could not take care of
its own poor. Other critics chastise her for not using her
great influence to help transform the unjust institutions
and oppressive structures that imprison so many in poverty. In addition, some theologians are critical of her language about Christ's renunciation of his filial identity on

the cross as well as her apparent embrace of suffering as a means of spiritual growth.

The church canonizes saints not because they were perfect but because they exemplify certain virtues worthy of imitation. Mother Teresa was not a theologian lauded for her orthodox Christology. She was not a social activist who challenged unjust structures and institutions. She did live the "great criterion" by helping individuals living on the streets of Calcutta to feel loved and to die embraced by love. It is possible to question the way St. Teresa described the relationship of Christ's thirst on the cross and the suffering of the poorest of the poor, but there is no doubt she practiced a Matthew 25 spirituality that included genuine solidarity with individual poor persons worthy of respect. She had a positive attitude toward poor persons, who are "great people," who "give us more than we give them," who need "love and compassion" more than pity, who "help us love God better," and who enable us "to contact Christ under his mask of wretchedness" with genuine joy.

We honor Mother Teresa as the Saint of Calcutta for good reasons: she saw Christ in the consecrated bread and wine at Mass and in the faces of the poorest of the poor; she personally cared for the dying, comforting them with a compassionate touch; she founded a religious order that serves a large number of poor people around the world; and she persevered through the dark night with a smile on her face.

An Unsung Saint

My own unsung model of merciful care for the needy is
my grade school classmate and lifelong friend, Pat, who,
very appropriately, is an exemplary member of the Sisters
of Mercy. Pat taught grade school and high school for
twenty-four years. She then served as a campus minster
for four years at Bowling Green State University, where
she went on to earn a doctorate with an excellent dissertation on liberation themes in the writings of the Black
author and activist James Baldwin. She then spent almost
thirty years as a professor of English at Siena Heights
University in Adrian, Michigan, teaching a variety of
courses, including Shakespeare, Black literature, and
Catholic short stories.

A Life of Service

Throughout her life as a Sister of Mercy, Pat has demonstrated special care for the least of our brothers and
sisters; for example, reaching out to troubled students in
her classes and leading students on numerous Christian
service missions to help needy youth in Jamaica. In addition, she has been a committed advocate for peace and justice, often joining public demonstrations against war (for
example, almost a year of frequent demonstrations against
the war in Iraq) and publishing letters to the editor and
Op-Ed articles in local papers in support of human rights
and just causes.

Advocating for a Felon

During her years at Siena Heights and beyond, Pat has taught weekly literature classes at a state prison just outside Adrian. In her short-story class, now almost thirty years ago, she was impressed with the intelligence and writing skills of a student, whom we will call "Bob." When he was seventeen years old, he was convicted of being an accessory to a murder and sentenced to "parolable life." After ten years in prison, Bob was denied parole despite being a model inmate and having a supportive family, an available residence, and a job awaiting him. Despondent and convinced he would never be paroled, Bob simply walked away from a minimum-security prison and spent six years working at a ranch in Texas before being apprehended and returned to prison.

It was a few years later that Pat met him in her class and committed herself to working for his release. Over the next twenty-five years, she persisted in this effort: writing to the parole board judge; sending petitions to the governor; meeting with congressmen; securing the services of a new, well-qualified lawyer; speaking on his behalf at two parole board hearings; soliciting the help of the governor's liaison to the state parole board; and speaking on Bob's behalf at a public hearing that led to his release after forty years in prison.

During her twenty-five-year effort, Pat visited Bob in prison several times and succeeded in getting a book of his short stories published. Ironically, during much of this time, Bob took out his frustrations on Pat, expressing his anger at her, accusing her of not doing enough, and berating her for engaging an incompetent lawyer to represent him. With prayerful reliance on divine help, Pat withstood this verbal abuse and maintained her commitment to free him from prison.

Since reentering society a few years ago, Bob has done well, with help from his family. He has stayed out of trouble, married a good woman, and written a novel. He and Pat have met a couple of times, and their conversations have been informative and cordial, although he has expressed nothing of an apology or gratitude. For her part, Pat continues to pray for him as she has for a quarter of a century.

Caring for the Homeless

The following story illumines Pat's commitment to helping the homeless. On Tuesday, December 20, 2005, a bitterly cold afternoon in Adrian, she was driving from the mall to the home she shared with three Dominican sisters. Pat saw a homeless man foraging in a garbage bag for pop and beer cans he could redeem for a dime apiece. She stopped, gave the man $20.00, all the money she had and sped home, where she spent hours sobbing, struck to the heart with guilt and dismay over the stark differences between her comfortable lifestyle and his homeless situation. At that moment, she vowed to do something to assist homeless persons in Adrian.

Pat started out by securing support from local churches and meeting regularly with interested pastors. She got an expert on homeless shelters in Ann Arbor to come to Adrian to give a presentation, which drew over 160 people and led to further meetings with a core group committed to the project. The group was able to open an overnight shelter, which they named "Share the Warmth," through January and February 2006, making use of space donated by two local Catholic churches. Pat not only led the planning but was also involved in the practical logistics of providing cots, blankets, and food, as well as recruiting and organizing volunteer helpers to supervise the shelter during the night.

As time went on, it became clear that assisting the homeless in Adrian required a larger facility. For two years, the Lutheran church provided a former school. After that, Pat entered into negotiations with a new Salvation Army captain that led to using their building to house Share the Warmth for the next eight winters. During these years, Pat helped move Share the Warmth toward a more structured organization with a governing board and official charitable status. Convinced that they needed a bigger and better building of their own, the board initiated a major fund-raising effort, including an annual dinner auction and golf tournament. Over time, they raised enough money to purchase the local Moose Lodge and can now house and feed up to sixty guests every day of the year.

In 2015, Pat retired from her teaching position at Siena Heights, handed over her coordinating role on the

board of Share the Warmth, and moved to her hometown of Toledo. However, she remains involved in Share
the Warmth, driving about thirty-five miles each way to
attend regular board meetings and spending all night,
about every two weeks, supervising the shelter, which
means getting little or no sleep. She continues to write
articles and give talks on justice and peace issues, while
maintaining her prison ministry in two separate facilities.

Prose Poems

In her marvelous book of prose poems, *Out of the Shadows*, Pat writes about Share the Warmth, where "need and
compassion intertwine," and where hosts not only feed
and shelter guests but look for simple ways to assist them,
like getting them to the store or church, and in more last-
ing ways, such as finding them a job and affordable hous-
ing. Citing the motto of the shelter, "Keeping people alive
until they can find hope," she speaks of "the hand that pro-
foundly joins hosts and guests" as they "huddle together,
always under the roof of God's mercy."

From that spiritual perspective, *Out of the Shadows*
presents ten prose poem profiles of individual guests who
have made an impact on Pat. For instance, there is

John

With grizzled beard and hair
and flaming eyes

he could be John the Baptist.
But this John booms slurred words
in alcoholic patois.
Layers of stained clothes
clutch his large frame
as he lies on his cot
in the corner of the Shelter.
When food arrives
he lumbers to the table
and begins cramming his mouth, oblivious to
    drops of spaghetti sauce
spotting his beard.
Once, thirty years ago
he took art classes at the college across town.
From alabaster stone
he sculpted a female figure
still displayed in the gallery's permanent
    exhibit.
He arouses a quixotic desire—
to take a hammer and chisel to him,
to chip away the boozy detritus of years
and uncover—like Michelangelo—
the stunning possibilities.

And there is

Anna

Anna's hair is long, thick, and straight,
a comely curtain

for her pretty plump face.
She chooses men badly.
Often she's sitting at the table
next to Bobby, sweet-faced alcoholic,
numb (it seems) to her arms
draped over his shoulders. Anna talks well
but has learning blocks and no GED.
Though she's tried.
A series of men
have all disappointed,
and last night at the shelter,
Bobby gruffly shoved her away
and collapsed onto his cot.
She sat and cried quietly, chest rippling with
        sobs.
Her children are with a relative.
Her heart is with the next man
who shows her kindness.
But she'll probably give Bobby
another chance.

For my friend Pat, the guests of Share the Warmth are not nameless, faceless street people in need of pity and patronizing assistance. On the contrary, as a true Sister of Mercy, she sees them as human beings with inherent dignity, as unique individuals with a distinctive story to tell, as children of a God who is ever merciful, and as the beloved of Christ, who identifies himself with the hungry and thirsty and all persons in need.

8

Discerning Our Path

Near the end of *Gaudete et Exultate*, Pope Francis has a section on "Discernment" (nos. 166–75), which enables us to recognize impulses from the Holy Spirit in a world of multiple options, various distractions, enticing novelties, dramatic events, and personal rigidity. For Francis, discernment is a gift of the Holy Spirit that we should develop through prayerful reflection, spiritual reading, and good counsel. To achieve genuine freedom in Christ, we need to examine the internal desires, anxieties, and questions in our own hearts as well as the external circumstances of our situation in the world. It is wise to use a prayerful discernment process not only in making big decisions in life but also in meeting our daily responsibilities. The pope highly recommends a daily examination of conscience as a valuable exercise in becoming a more discerning person. An effective discernment takes into account psychological and sociological factors as well as church teaching, but transcends them by seeking a graced "glimpse of that unique and mysterious plan that God has for each on us" (no. 170). We should consider not only our temporal well-being, personal satisfaction, and peace of mind but also the meaning of our life before the Father, who knows and loves us. Discernment is a gift available to everyone that requires no special ability but only the effort to develop it as best we can. In this process, we need periods of silence to calm our anxieties and interpret our impulses from a faith perspective. We need to listen to the realities of life, to the good advice of others, and to the voice of the Lord, all of which can challenge our ordinary ways of seeing things and "shatter our security but lead us to a better life."

Discerning Christians accept the gospel "as the ultimate standard" and respect the church teaching that interprets it. They do not merely apply rules or repeat past approaches but stay open to the risen Lord and the Spirit, who alone can "penetrate what is obscure and hidden in every situation" so that "the newness of the Gospel can emerge in another light." In this process, it helps to remember the patience of God, whose timetable is not ours, and to accept the "logic of the cross," which calls us to self-sacrificing love for others. Francis concludes his deep and insightful analysis: "Discernment, then, is not a solipsistic self-analysis or a form of egotistical introspection, but an authentic process of leaving ourselves behind in order to approach the mystery of God, who helps us to carry out the mission to which he has called us, for the good of our brothers and sisters" (no. 175).

A CELEBRATED SAINT

Saint John Henry Newman (1801–1890), cardinal of the church, can serve as a celebrated example of a discerning Christian who sought to do God's will and wrote insightful analyses of the process. John Henry was born on February 21, 1801, in London, the son of a banker and the oldest of five siblings. At the age of seven, his parents sent him to Great Ealing School, a private boarding school, where he studied mathematics and classical Greek and Latin texts. Around the age of fifteen, he had a striking, unmistakable religious experience through which he "fell under the influence of a definite creed" and gained a sense of the importance of church dogma, which stayed with him the rest of his life. When he was only seventeen, he enrolled in Trinity College, Oxford, where he studied intently for two years but performed far below expectations on his final exams, barely passing to earn a bachelor of arts degree. Embarrassed but resolute, he continued his studies and, in 1822, did so well in a grueling set of exams that he was elected a fellow of Oriel College, his dream job, which he later described as the turning point in his life and the fulfillment of his academic ambitions. Now securely set for life with a guaranteed income, lodging, and food, Newman devoted himself to an academic career of teaching, researching, writing, and tutoring students. He also gradually became more involved in the Anglican Church, which led to his ordination as a priest in 1825 and an appointment three years later as vicar of St. Mary's

University Church, where he regularly preached long and thoughtful sermons that attracted widespread interest.

Oxford Movement

Starting around 1833, Newman, along with John Keble and Edwin Pusey, led what came to be known as the Oxford Movement, designed to reform the Church of England by resisting its tilt toward Protestantism and incorporating more Roman Catholic thought and practice. Newman, who exercised influence on both the content and the strategy of the movement, edited *Tracts for the Times* (1833–1841), consisting of a series of ninety tracts, and personally wrote twenty-four of them on specific ecclesial issues. His famous Tract 90 (1841) claimed that the fundamental beliefs of the Anglican Church, expressed in the Thirty-nine Articles officially adopted in 1571, were in accord with the teachings of the early church and the Council of Trent (1545–1563). This tract generated intense reactions among Anglicans who felt it was too accommodating to the Roman Church. It moved the Anglican bishop of Oxford, with the consent of the archbishop of Canterbury, to prohibit any further publication of the tracts. Newman refused to disavow the content of Tract 90, but accepted the order of his bishop to discontinue the series of tracts, fortified by the conviction that the ideas were now public and would eventually bear fruit in renewing the Church of England.

Doubts

In the summer of 1839, John Henry Newman, in the course of his research, began for the first time to have doubts about "the tenableness of Anglicanism" that initiated a six-year discernment process leading to his conversion to the Roman Catholic Church in 1845. In his *Apologia pro Vita Sua*, published decades later, Newman gives us a glimpse of the discernment process that led to his conversion. He describes an initial "vivid impression on his intellect" that "the Church of Rome will be found right after all," which faded away but left him with an imperative to learn more about the Roman Church and to use his reason to judge the validity of this intuition. For him, prayer was essential to the process, as he asked God "to reveal Himself" more fully and to "guide me with His counsel." He was ready to undertake the process of following God's will one step at a time, as he wrote in his famous poem, "Lead Kindly Light," which has the significant verse: "I do not ask to see/The distant scene; one step enough for me." In this gradual process, he was committed to discerning God's will and using reason to determine the validity of his imaginative intuitions.

Issues

During his long conversion process, Newman had to make choices about specific issues. For example, he wrestled with the question of remaining as the vicar of St. Mary's

University Church, while experiencing so many doubts. On the one hand, he questioned his pastoral effectiveness, noting that he did not have many close relationships with his parishioners, and many of the programs he established ended up serving the university more than the parish. Furthermore, he admitted that his peaching was not directed to defending Anglicanism but to drawing on the wisdom of the primitive church to guide moral decision making, which he feared might dispose the congregation to more favorable attitudes toward the Roman Church. In dealing with these doubts and fears, Newman prayed for guidance and sought advice from persons he trusted to share his personal misgivings. In 1841, he ended up following the advice of a friend to maintain his position, trusting that his preaching could further the cause of Anglican reform and even serve as a "providential means of uniting the whole church in one." The fact that he was assigned a curate who took on much of the pastoral duties eased his conscience and strengthened his resolve to do his best as vicar of St. Mary's.

Defending Anglicanism

In the beginning of the section in his *Apologia* on the years 1841 to 1845, Newman states that by the end of 1841 he was "on my deathbed as regards my membership with the Anglican Church, though at the time I became aware of it only by degrees." He goes on to describe his intellectual efforts during this period to determine if the four notes or marks of the early church (one, holy, catholic, and apostolic) were kept alive in the Church of England or were more fully present in the Roman Catholic Church, as he eventually concluded. As a practicing Anglican priest and preacher, however, Newman saw the Church of England as a branch of the one true church, along with Orthodox Christianity and Roman Catholicism. For him, Anglicanism was a *via media*, a middle way between Protestantism and Catholicism that preserved the apostolic succession of its hierarchy and remained a source of holiness for its members. During that period, Newman wrote extensively in support of the Church of England and in criticism of the Church of Rome, including its teaching on transubstantiation and its practice of excessive devotion to Mary.

Role of Imagination

Newman's *Apologia* contains many clues to his discernment process. He tells us that, despite "his ingrained distrust of Rome" and his "affection for Oxford and Oriel," he had a "secret longing love of Rome" and a "true devotion to the Blessed Virgin." In response to the charges made by his critic Charles Kingsley and others that he was dishonest in his public statements, Newman defended his own integrity: "I have never had any suspicion of my own honesty." In his quest for the truth, he was not so much moved by logical reason as by imagination, which envisions the future, makes connections, and incorporates personal developments. He simply found himself as a "whole man" moving toward Rome and away from the Church of England.

Self-Criticism

Newman's study of the fourth-century Arian heresy forced him to abandon his position that Anglicanism was a legitimate middle way between the Orthodox and Roman churches and led him to the disturbing conclusion that the contemporary Church of England reflected the position of the heretical semi-Arians. His eventual disavowal of Anglicanism led Newman to a serious self-examination of his many faulty affirmations and defenses of that tradition. He concluded that his fundamental error was to accept uncritically the teachings of the Anglican divines—church scholars like Jeremy Taylor—without personally studying the validity of their positions, thus simply repeating some of their misreadings of the apostolic tradition. He was, in his own words, "careless" in his approach, exercising "more faith than criticism" on matters of crucial importance to his quest for truth. At the same time, he believed that changing his opinion on Anglicanism would "issue in the triumph of liberalism," the "anti-dogmatic principle" that effectively denies the validity of all truth claims. The thought that rejecting the truth of the Anglican tradition would somehow foster the liberalism he fought his whole life was "oppressive" to him and made him extremely unhappy, especially if it led some of his friends and followers to leave the Church of England and join the liberal movement.

In response to critics who claimed that he stayed in the English Church too long after his doubts arose, Newman points out that he did not leave the church in 1841 because there was still a chance that his doubts could be solved. He chose, instead, to remain an Anglican, but to give up his clerical duties as vicar of St. Mary's and return to Littlemore, where he lived a simple monastic life for two years. He vigorously denied the charge that during those years he was a "concealed Romanist" who already converted and insisted that he did not seek to harm the English Church in any way.

Newman's discernment process also included his efforts to make sense of his growing "sympathies" for the religion of Rome as well as his ongoing problems with some Roman doctrines, such as transubstantiation, a teaching on how Christ was present in the Eucharist that he did not find in the apostolic teaching. He was also troubled by the practice of Marian devotions, which seemed excessive to him at the time.

The Development of Doctrine

In 1843, to deal with the additions to the traditional creed found in the Roman Church, Newman began an intense study of the development of doctrine, which led to the 1845 publication of his book *An Essay on the Devel-*

opment of Christian Doctrine. For Newman, Christian doctrines are valid and accurate, if imperfect and limited, verbal expressions of the living faith, which have their life and meaning in a real commitment to Christ. Doctrines develop as Christian faith itself develops in response to changing circumstances and new challenges. Doctrines are true if they are faithful to the fuller meaning of Scripture and tradition and are relevant if they convey that meaning in changing circumstances. The Christian community possesses an "intuition of faith," grounded and sustained by God's grace and guided by creeds and liturgy, which itself develops as Christians live their faith in new historical and cultural contexts. Newman used this theological framework to examine developments in Roman Catholicism and to argue in favor of "the identity of Roman and Primitive Christianity," which cleared away a major obstacle to joining the Catholic Church.

Religious Certitude

To make this tremendously consequential move, Newman had to explain how to achieve certitude in matters of faith and religion, an issue that he began to study at the time of his conversion and completed early in 1870 with the publication of his *An Essay in Aid of a Grammar of Assent.* Commenting on his state of belief in 1844, he said his belief in God, Christianity, and Catholicism was based on a "cumulative transcendent probability," a type of certitude that rises higher than our logical conclusions. He made his decision to become a Catholic on the grounds of "converging probabilities" that the English Church was wrong and the Roman Church was right.

Moving toward Rome

In 1843, Newman issued a "Formal Retraction" of all the "hard things" he said against the Church of Rome, explaining that his previous statements followed "almost a consensus" of the Anglican divines, but admitting that he was influenced by his own "impetuous temper," his desire to please persons he respected, and his "wish to repel the charge of Romanism." Against the critics who said that he should not have published his critical views of Rome, he defended himself by arguing that publishing was a better option than silence and that publishing the *Tracts* defending Anglicanism demanded an accompanying protest against Rome to be effective.

By May 1843, Newman wrote a friend that as well as he could analyze his own convictions, he considered "the Roman Catholic Communion to be the Church of the Apostles" and that "the English Church was in schism." In September 1843, he resigned as vicar of St. Mary's, leaving him with only one more "advance of mind to make," to be certain of his conviction and to actually submit to the Catholic Church, which he did two years later in 1845.

Revealing His Convictions

In the meantime, he wrestled with questions of revealing his convictions and intentions to various individuals. He also did not want to unsettle anyone, and so he "said nothing to anyone," unless obliged. He wished to go to the Lord by himself, in his own way, without taking others with him. In a letter to a friend on October 25, 1843, Newman disclosed his preference for the Church of Rome and his trust that God who has kept me "in the slow course of change" will "keep me still from hasty acts or resolves with a doubtful conscience." He informed his friend that their correspondence relieved him of "a heavy secret," took away "the pain of disclosure," and suggested "traces of a Providential Hand." And yet, he never told a dying dear friend of his state of mind, even when asked, because he did not yet have certitude on his direction and did not want to unsettle a man calmly facing death.

His Conversion

In 1845, as Newman made progress on the issue of doctrinal development, his "view so cleared" that he resolved to be received into what he now boldly called not the Roman Church but "the Catholic Church." On October 8, 1845, he wrote to a number of friends that he intended that very night to ask Fr. Dominic Barbier, a Passionist, to admit him into "the one Fold of Christ," which was accomplished the next day, October 9, which is now the date of his feast day as a canonized saint in the Catholic liturgical calendar.

After His Conversion

Reflecting on his experiences after his conversion, Newman wrote in the beginning of chapter 5 of his *Apologia* that he had "no anxiety of heart," enjoyed "perfect peace and contentment," and never had "one doubt." He was not conscious of any "inward difference of thought," or "firmer faith in the fundamental truths of revelation" or "more self-command" or "more fervor." Rather, "it was like coming into port after a rough sea; and my happiness on that score remains to this day without interruption." Newman tells us he had no trouble accepting Catholic doctrines that went beyond the Anglican Church, even though he could not answer all the difficulties they presented, famously noting that "ten thousand difficulties do not make one doubt." For example, he had no trouble accepting the Catholic teaching on transubstantiation after he joined the Catholic Church, even though he had not personally researched all aspects of the question.

After his conversion, Newman was ordained a Catholic priest, joined the Oratorian order, founded an oratory in Birmingham, England, helped establish the Catholic University of Ireland, where he served as its first rector, and published important books, including *The Idea of a University* and *The Grammar of Assent*.

Before the First Vatican Council in 1870, Newman

spoke out against proclaiming the doctrine of papal infallibility but accepted it when the council promulgated it. In 1879, Pope Leo XIII appointed him a cardinal of the church, which, as Newman noted, lifted the suspicion that he was a heretic who could not be trusted. His chosen motto, *Cor ad cor loquitur* (Heart speaks to heart), reminds us today of the interpersonal aspects of the discernment process.

Analyzing Discernment

Not only did John Henry Newman live a long, complex, prayerful discernment process leading to his conversion, but his thoughtful reflections on the process can be organized into didactic pairs that can guide our efforts today to live as discerning Christians in the contemporary world. For example, he fruitfully combined a passion for the high ideals of holiness with practical efforts to live the faith in the ordinary events of life. He was totally committed to doing God's will, to becoming the best person he could be, to seeking truth wholeheartedly, and to making a constructive impact on the world. At the same time, he believed in taking one step at a time, as we saw in his most famous poem, "Lead Kindly Light": "I do not ask to see/The distant scene; one step enough for me." He advises, "If we would aim at perfection, we must perform well the duties of the day. I do not know anything more difficult, more sobering, so strengthening, than the constant aim to go through the ordinary days well." The hallmark of a truly spiritual person is an unpretentious consistency and carefulness in meeting daily responsibilities, including small distasteful duties. Newman encourages us to remember "how mysteriously little things are in this world connected with great: how simple moments, improved or wasted, are the salvation or ruin of all-important interests." He warns us how difficult it is to be "disciplined and regular in our religion." While it is very easy to be religious by "fits and starts" and to excite our feelings by "artificial stimulants," but regular practice seems to "trammel us and we become impatient."

For Newman, the passion for holiness and the dedication to daily fidelity are rooted in the commitment to do the will of God, who walks with us as we discern the next step on the path to greater spiritual maturity. It is the loving God who calls us to maintain our high ideals despite our limitations and failures and to practice our faith on a daily basis despite distractions and other demands. In discerning our path to holiness, we do well to maintain a dialectical tension between high ideals and the demands of everyday life.

Relating Doctrine and Experience

During his lifelong spiritual journey, Newman maintained a healthy respect for both official church doctrines and his own personal religious experience. The deep experience he had at age fifteen, when he "fell under the influence of a definite creed" and received into his intellect "impressions of dogma," remained with him throughout his life. This enduring conviction fostered his lifelong battle against religious liberalism that displayed a "real antipathy or anger against revealed truth." At the same time, his study of the Arian heresy taught him the limitations of church dogmas that are only "the shadow projected for the contemplation of the intellect" of the ultimately mysterious God. They are "necessarily imperfect" representations exhibited "in a foreign medium" of the object of our spiritual search. However, church doctrines, limited as they are, do assist us in our "acts of religious worship and obedience."

One of Newman's most creative and significant contributions to modern theology is his classic study of the development of Christian doctrine, which, as we saw, was a crucial part of his discernment process leading to his acceptance of Catholic teaching. For him, doctrines develop in an organic way, as Christians, challenged by new situations and questions, draw new conclusions out of the original faith. He worked out seven criteria for valid developments: preserving the original essential truth; keeping the same fundamental principles; assimilating new elements into the understanding of the faith; drawing new conclusions from its principles; recognizing that the earlier understanding anticipated the later developments; being faithful to the original principles in new circumstances; and maintaining the spiritual energy and tenacity of the original faith.

Newman joined his enduring appreciation of church

doctrine with a modern interest and trust in his God-guided personal religious experiences. He learned important lessons from his travels, especially from his later reflections on them. The serious illness that he experienced when he was fifteen helped solidify his Christian faith and led him to the conviction that his "calling in life would require such a sacrifice as celibacy involved." The death of his beloved sister, Mary, moved the twenty-seven-year-old John Henry to develop a strong sense of the "transitory nature of this world" and to experience "subtle feelings" that sickened his soul but helped him see his sister "embodied" in the beautiful things of this world.

Newman did not have a particularly striking conversion experience but did speak of "a returning to, a renewing of principles under the power of the Holy Spirit," which he had already experienced in his youth. For him, faith involved a deep personal assent to the truth of revelation but always formed and facilitated by the church and its official teaching. In our world today, Newman invites sincere searchers who value their personal experience to consider the positive role church doctrines can play in encouraging and guiding spiritual development.

Authority

We can find further guidance on effective discernment by examining the way Newman related the authority of the church and the conscience of individuals. Throughout his life, this great scholar demonstrated great respect for authority in both the Anglican and the Catholic churches. For example, despite his passion for renewing the Church of England, he submitted to the bishop of Oxford who halted the publication of the *Tracts*, the ninety pamphlets that were such an effective means of spreading the Oxford Movement. As a Catholic, he worked within the hierarchical structure: for example, getting permission from Rome to found an Oratory in Birmingham, England. He tried to work with the Irish bishops in founding a Catholic University in Dublin, despite his lack of support and many disagreements with the Irish cardinals. He was opposed to the promulgation of papal infallibility at the First Vatican Council in 1870, but after it was officially adopted, he vigorously defended it, while noting its limitations. He was critical of the way the teaching on infallibility was pushed through the council and remained respectful of the views of the bishops who left the council in protest before the vote.

In general, Newman emphasized the limitations of papal power. He thought it was not healthy for a pope to reign for a long time, as Pius IX did, for over thirty-eight years. He predicted a future council would place papal power in a larger context, as Vatican II actually did by its teaching on collegiality. He favored the enlargement of the College of Cardinals and thought the papacy should be open to other nationalities. For him, the hierarchy was a proper and necessary part of the church structure, but it must be balanced by the work of the theologians and the lived spirituality of the baptized.

Conscience

Newman balanced this nuanced view of church authority with a strong emphasis on the role of individual conscience. It is through our conscience that we know the will of God and follow the divine law implanted in our intelligence. Our conscience, properly informed by Scripture and church teaching, is our proximate norm for making moral decisions about what we should do and not do. We form our conscience on specific issues by "serious thought, prayer, and all available means of arriving at a right judgment on the matter in question." Newman insisted that we are obliged to act on our properly informed conscience, even if it is not in total accord with church authority, convinced as he was that fidelity to conscience and a passion for truth do eventually lead us to God. Commenting on an obligation to bring religion into an after-dinner toast, Newman famously said he would drink to the pope, "still, to Conscience first and to the Pope afterwards." Clearly, this priority for conscience must be seen in its dialectical relationship to authority, which is rooted in the common task of pursuing God's will. Authority protects individuals from subjectivism, from making faulty decisions based only on self-interest. Conscience interprets general authoritative teaching and applies it to concrete decision making. Given the immense influence of individualism in our culture, it seems especially important to bring objective criteria into our personal effort to discern our unique path to holiness.

The canonization of St. John Henry Newman has generated greater interest in his life and thought. His journey from Anglicanism to Catholicism is a remarkably concrete example of a discernment process guided by prayer and a commitment to following God's will. His creative dialectical theology contains wise advice for us today, suggesting we take into account in discerning our spiritual path both high ideals and humble means, both Christian doctrines and personal experience, and both church authority and individual conscience.

An Unsung Saint

I see elements of a graced discernment process in the story of a faithful Catholic woman by the name of Charmaine, who was born in the late 1930s in Sandusky, Ohio, a twin with an older sister. She was raised in a good Catholic family that faithfully attended Mass on Sundays and Holy Days, prayed before meals, went to Lenten services, and participated in popular Catholic devotions. As an adult, she remembers with gratitude that a charitable atmosphere prevailed in her family, with no harsh language or swearing. While attending St. Mary's grade school and high school, Charmaine was taught by the Sisters of Notre Dame, who gained her admiration for instilling the Catholic faith in their students. After graduation from high school, she took a job at the local Catholic hospital, Providence, setting aside her thoughts of becoming a nurse, since that would put a strain on her parents' finances. Grateful for her job, she saw herself on the normal path of most of her friends, which would lead to getting married and raising a family.

A Dilemma

It was in 1958 that Charmaine first met Tom, a young man her age, who came from the nearby town of Fremont to socialize with friends at a local hangout in Sandusky. When she first met Tom, something told her he was "the one." They began dating, getting together during weekends, enjoying movies, sporting events, bowling, and spending time with friends and family. As time went on, they talked religion, and Charmaine learned that Tom's Lutheran church was really important to him. Since some of Tom's Lutheran friends converted to marry Catholic girls, she assumed he would do the same. However, it gradually became clear that he was as committed to maintaining his Lutheran faith as she was to remaining Catholic.

Thus began a long ten-year discernment process for both of them. They were deeply in love, enjoyed each other's company, and had so much in common. They shared fundamental Christian teachings and moral principles. They did not live together but stayed with their own families, who were both welcoming and enthusiastic about the potential addition to their family. After extensive conversations, their respective positions became clear: Charmaine, on the one hand, would definitely not give up her Catholic faith and would continue to practice it. She wanted to be married in her parish church but would be willing to have her children raised Lutheran. Tom, on the other hand, was totally committed to his Lutheran church, where he and his family were very involved, and was adamantly opposed to raising his children Catholic.

During their long discernment process, Tom spent two years in military service. After returning home, he gave Charmaine an engagement ring, which she accepted without knowing how things could get worked out. Her parents and siblings, who loved Tom, supported her with love but did not offer any advice. One of Charmaine's Catholic friends encouraged her to give in, leave the Catholic Church, marry Tom, and become a Lutheran. This left Charmaine in turmoil, as she just could not imagine leaving the Catholic Church, which was so important to her.

At some point, in my role as assistant pastor for St. Mary's Parish, I met Charmaine at Providence Hospital during my regular visits to the sick. As she got to know me better, she told me her story and asked my advice. We set up a meeting with Tom and his pastor, which involved a long, intense, honest, charitable, and prayerful dialogue, but yielded no solutions. Charmaine was disappointed, but continued to pray that Tom would convert. She prayed at Mass, said the rosary, and developed a deep devotion to St. Jude, the apostle and patron of lost causes. I was very familiar with this devotion since my family regularly went after Sunday Mass to a shrine of St. Jude to pray for my younger brother, David, who was totally disabled from birth due to the complications of Rh disease. I marveled at the faith and tenacity of Charmaine and felt a kinship with her reliance on prayer and devotion to St. Jude. At one point, Tom wanted to give up, but Charmaine prayed to St. Jude and found the words to encourage him not to lose hope. I continued to stay in touch with Charmaine, seeing her periodically and regularly praying for her and Tom.

A Solution

In 1968, my bishop sent me to New York for further studies, where I was privileged to study under some of the best international theologians, including the great Redemptorist moral theologian Bernard Häring, who had close ties to some key curial officials in Rome. I presented Charmaine's case to him, and he showed me how to write a petition to Rome asking permission for her to get married in the Catholic Church, while promising to raise her children "ecumenically," the key word that would win Vatican approval of the marriage. Sure enough, within months, the Vatican sent official permission for the marriage; and in 1968, after ten years of intense discernment, Charmaine and Tom were married in St. Mary's Church and settled in Fremont, Tom's hometown. They came to see me in New York on their honeymoon, and we said prayers of gratitude over a joyous dinner.

Charmaine and Tom have enjoyed a long and happy marriage without ever having any conflicts over religion. Charmaine got involved in Sacred Heart Catholic Church, where she attends Mass regularly on Saturdays. She cooperated closely with Tom in raising their three children in the Lutheran Church, and during that time attended services every Sunday at St. Mark Lutheran Church. In 2018, they celebrated their fiftieth wedding anniversary, filled with gratitude for God's blessing of a wonderful Christian marriage.

Application

For me, Charmaine remains an inspiring example of a committed Catholic who practiced important elements of a graced discernment process. She was faithful to her informed conscience and acted on principle rather than expediency; she tried to do God's will and relied on regular prayer; she sought guidance and engaged in respectful dialogue; she tried to understand the obstacles and persevered in seeking viable solutions; she trusted her deep love of Tom and respected his own religious commitments and moral integrity; finally, she rejoiced in the surprising solution as a gift from God and remained faithful to her promise to live her Catholic faith and to raise her children ecumenically. It seems proper to note that their story told from Tom's perspective would also reveal his deep faith and prayerful discernment process.

I have on numerous occasions shared the story of Tom and Charmaine with couples contemplating an ecumenical marriage, reminding them that fidelity to conscience is crucial to making a successful marriage and encouraging them to make decisions about how to raise their children religiously before getting married and not waiting until it is time to baptize the first child. Over the years, Tom and Charmaine have assured me that they are glad that their story has helped other couples trying to discern the path to a happy and holy marriage. Now my hope is that their permission to retell their inspiring story will provide guidance and encouragement to others striving to discern God's will in various circumstances.

Signposts and Principles

These chapters, based on the apostolic exhortation *Gaudium et Exultate* of Pope Francis, provide helpful signposts for saints and general principles for spiritual development.

1. We are all called by God to become our better selves, to actualize our potential, to grow spiritually, and to become a saint. *Advice*: do not get deterred by the idealistic language of sainthood but find an effective motivation for doing your best and rising above mediocrity.
2. We must discover our own unique path to holiness based on our gifts, interests, and circumstances. *Advice*: do not try to imitate others or compare your spiritual progress with theirs.
3. Our path to greater spiritual maturity passes through our everyday lives and our ordinary activities. *Advice*: avoid the common traps of waiting for a spectacular intervention by God and expecting to become more spiritual when less busy and stressed.
4. We grow spiritually by deepening our personal relationship with Christ and committing ourselves to fol-

lowing his example and teaching. *Advice*: find a way to view Christ as the decisive figure in your life; for example, the only Son of God, the Supreme Paradigm of full humanity, the Lord of the entire cosmos, the definitive Prophet, the Savior of the whole human family, or the greatest moral Teacher.

5. Our effort to live the Christian life must include the pursuit of justice for the most vulnerable. *Advice*: remember that injustice gets embedded in systems and institutions; follow the consistent ethic of life that seeks the protection and flourishing of human beings in all stages of development and in all forms of marginalization; do all you can in your own circle of influence, even if you see little progress.

6. Our spiritual journey is enhanced by maintaining a contemplative spirit in the midst of a busy active life. *Advice*: reserve time for daily prayer and meditation, which provide motivation and energy for meeting your daily responsibilities.

7. We are all called to follow the teachings of Christ by extending mercy to those in need. *Advice*: reflect on the passage in Matthew 25:31–46, where Jesus identifies himself with persons who are hungry, thirsty, strangers, naked, sick, and imprisoned; remember this is the "great criterion" for getting to heaven.

8. We all need to develop the gift of discernment in making wise decisions about our vocation in life and following God's will in our everyday lives. *Advice*: consider your gifts and talents, your internal interests and

desires, as well as external opportunities and challenges; stay faithful to the spiritual practices of prayerful reflection, spiritual reading, and examination of
conscience; do not simply follow rules but stay open to
the promptings of the Holy Spirit, who guides us to do
God's will and follow the example of Christ.

Pope Francis is indeed a wise spiritual director for the
whole Christian world, and his beautifully written apostolic exhortation is an important contribution to contemporary spirituality that deserves our attention.

Further Reading

Primary

Augustine, Saint. *The Confessions.* Translated by Maria Boulding, OSB. Hyde Park, NY: New City Press, 2002.

Francis, Pope. *Gaudete et Exultate* ("On the Call to Holiness in Today's World"). vatican.va.

Francis of Assisi, Saint. "The Canticle of Creation" (c. 1224). https://www.catholic.org/prayers.

Hammarskjöld, Dag. *Markings.* Translated by Leif Sjoberg and W. H. Auden. New York: Vintage Books, 2006.

Ignatius, Saint. *Spiritual Exercises of St. Ignatius.* Translated by George E. Ganss. Chicago: Loyola Press, 1992.

King, Martin Luther, Jr. "I've Been to the Mountaintop." Last speech, delivered April 3, 1968, at Mason Temple in Memphis, Tennessee. http://www.speeches-usa.com.

———. "The Montgomery Bus Boycott." Speech delivered at the Holt Street Baptist Church in Montgomery, Alabama, on December 5, 1955. https://www.black past.org.

Newman, John Henry Cardinal. *Apologia pro Vita Sua.* New York: E. P. Dutton, 1864.

——. *An Essay in Aid of a Grammar of Assent.* London: Longmans, Green, 1903.

——. *An Essay on the Development of Christian Doctrine.* London: Longmans, Green, 1909.

——. *The Idea of a University.* London: Longmans, Green, 1907.

——. "The Pillar of the Cloud." In *Newman Reader: Works of John Henry Newman.* Pittsburgh, PA: National Institute for Newman Studies, 2007.

——. *Tracts for the Times.* South Bend, IN: University of Notre Dame Press, 2013.

Thérèse of Lisieux, Saint. *Story of a Soul: The Autobiography of St. Therese of Lisieux.* Translated by John Clarke, 3rd edition. Washington, DC: ICS Publications, 1996.

Secondary

Bacik, James. *Apologetics and the Eclipse of Mystery: Mystagogy According to Karl Rahner.* South Bend, IN: University of Notre Dame Press, 1980.

——. *Pope Francis and Campus Ministry.* Mahwah, NJ: Paulist Press, 2019.

——. *Pope Francis and His Critics.* Mahwah, NJ: Paulist Press, 2020.

Farrell, Edward J. *Prayer Is a Hunger.* Denville, NJ: Dimension Books, 1972.

Leidorf, Ruth Ann, and Bernard J. Boff. *Surprises of the Spirit: Lessons Learned from Experience and the Word.* Toledo, OH: Mission of Accompaniment, 2004.

Lipsey, Roger. *Hammarskjöld: A Life.* Ann Arbor, MI: University of Michigan Press, 2013.

Merton, Thomas. *Conjectures of a Guilty Bystander.* New York: Image, 1968.

——. *The Seven Storey Mountain.* New York: Harcourt, 1976.

Mother Teresa. *Mother Teresa: Come Be My Light.* Edited by Brian Kolodiejchuk. New York: Image, 2013.

Nouwen, Henry. *The Return of the Prodigal Son.* New York: Doubleday, 1992.

——. *The Wounded Healer.* New York: Image, 1979.

Radler, Charlotte. "In Love I Am More God: The Centrality of Love in Meister Eckhart's Mysticism." *Journal of Religion* 90, no. 2 (2010): 171–98.

Rahner, Karl. *Foundations of Christian Faith.* Translated by William V. Dych. New York: Seabury Press, 1978.

Thompson, Francis. "The Hound of Heaven." In D. H. S. Nicholson and A. H. E. Lee, eds., *The Oxford Book of English Mystical Verse.* Oxford: Clarendon Press, 1917; bartleby.com, 2000. www.bartleby.com/236/.